Race to
Acceptance

Race to
Acceptance

Denise O'Connor

authorHOUSE®

AuthorHouse™ UK Ltd.
1663 Liberty Drive
Bloomington, IN 47403 USA
www.authorhouse.co.uk
Phone: 0800.197.4150

Published by AuthorHouse   07/01/2013

ISBN: 978-1-4817-6888-7 (sc)
ISBN: 978-1-4817-6859-7 (hc)
ISBN: 978-1-4817-6889-4 (e)

CHAPTER 1

THE UNKNOWN

Wise folk out there would advise us that if we ask questions along the way and we take in all the relevant information around us and try to make the right decisions, then, we do not have to worry. Is this actually what we do or how we come to decide on one thing and not on another? What if you ask the question; 'Am I fulfilled in every way and do I feel like I am really living at the moment? Without doubting that enlightenment was very far away, I asked it one day and I found that I needed a push in order to believe that I was really living. I wasn't really sure what that meant, to be honest. First, I thought I needed a man, but that hadn't gone to plan before, so I quickly reminded myself that personal contentment does not come from other people. Then I concentrated on the material things that society deemed 'appropriate' to have now that I was in my late 20's. The first very important, truly Irish factor was the proverbial 'house ladder' of the early noughties which I tended to walk under rather than up! It is funny when we think of all these pressures put on us from a society we just happened to be born into and I felt that need to conform. After that, I didn't know what it was that was 'missing' from my life but something was not quite right. I did, however, realise quite early on that neither men nor property were going to fulfil this in any way.

I had come out of a somewhat troubled relationship months before and I was trying to move on. I had all this pent up energy inside of me (both positive and negative) and I needed to direct it in a productive way. I was spending my nights out on the 'scene' drinking with new found friends and staying out all night just so I wouldn't have to be alone at home, forced to think about the direction my life was going and edging myself into corners on decisions which were on a foot long finger. I was lost as they say.

I couldn't tell anyone what was wrong because I hadn't even had that conversation with myself. To the outside world (and the outer me) there was nothing wrong. I could have gone on like that forever. It was fun, somewhere in there. Wild nights, late mornings, freedom.

The hangovers wore off and what was left was a long way from that freedom!

I have never really understood why, in the end, I chose to spend 'a few months'searching for something that only language in the self-help section of a bookshop would get away with. It was the stereotypical idea of helping the poor and appreciating my life more. People ask me now why I chose this unknown country and why I chose to go there at this time in my life. It is very strange. It just came to me one evening. I was sitting watching some mind numbing rubbish on the television and this thought popped into my head—I needed space and Ghana was the place to find it!

To be honest, I had never really heard of this country and all I knew was that they had a decent national football team and they exported a lot of cocoa. Apparently, this was a hell of a lot more than what others around me knew! For a long time, everyone would say 'Ghana? Wow, South America, that's great'. I realised there was a country called 'Guyana', which did sound like my African far away green hill. I did get some hilarious reactions to be decision, especially from my old buddies in Howth, where we had perched ourselves together at some of the bars there for years putting the world to right over pints and cigarettes. Now, I was leaving, past Sutton Cross and off to a country we had never even discussed!

The clichéd civilian mission I had set for myself became more of a reality for me as time went on.

I was a language teacher at the time at the time and I did feel I had enough experience and qualifications to offer my services in Ghana. I went to USIT and interviewed for a place on the VSO (Voluntary Services Overseas) programme. I was offered it there and then and began my preparations to leave.

I was given a contact liaison person in Accra, the capital who would organise a host family for me and a work placement at a local school. This sounded like a great arrangement at the time! I prepared by getting my visa from the Ghanaian Consulate, giving notice at the school I worked in and packing my bags. I remember being so concerned about what to pack, torn between my mini skirts and conservative clothing.

What lay ahead of me now was a mystery and I felt that I would leave for the 6 months, get my head together and return home.

Having asked whether I was fully awake and living, (an idea from the book 'Awareness' by Anthony De Melllo, the great Jesuit priest and psychotherapist) a decision was made to board a plane to Ghana, which I knew was somewhere in the West of Africa and the previous United Nations Secretary General, Kofi Annan, was from there!

The engines roared that little bit more, my hands clasped the side of the seat and off went flight LH564 en route to Kotoka airport, Accra, Ghana, West Africa!

With my nerves soaring as high as the aircraft, I thought about the world I was going to spend the next 6 months in. Alone, feeling suddenly very aware of my pale skin and western tendencies for the first time in my life, I thought of the country lying ahead. I was diving deep into a new realm, embarking on a journey involving the discovery of an education process on this side of the world. As an English teacher,

I thought I would take my experience and put it to good use as many others have done in the past. If I had known then how much this ego-driven, thirst for adventure quenching was going to change my life, there is a chance I may have been on a package holiday at that moment. Or, maybe, as faith would have it, what was destined to happen would happen anyway.

So, what did I really know about the new world I was so willing to become part of?

On paper, I was well prepared.

Ghana has a population of twenty three million and lies in West Africa. As a teacher, I had a particular interest in the education system in the African continent and now, specifically Ghana. I was fascinated by how education played a part in combating poverty or, even, what was the relationship between education, poverty and economic progression. Are children been given enough to make changes happen or do they even want them? These were similar questions I would ask about the system in Ireland and hoped one day to do a PhD focusing on this very area.

During my stay, I would not claim to be an expert in the entire education system of Ghana, or indeed even in the small area I delved into, but I tried to stay as objective and observant as possible. Having done an MA in Intercultural Studies in DCU, I had studies a lot on ethnography, where anthropologists (and others) travel to different parts of the world studying other cultures and writing about them. This was what I really wanted to do but neither time nor money were on my side and it is hard to pitch this kind of activity as a 'career' at home! We would study people like Malinowski who studied people in Papua New Guinea and Colin Turnbull who lived with the Mbuti tribe in the Congo. This was all going through my mind as I attempted to sieve through this unknown world.

Education, as we all know, is a huge spectrum spanning from kindergarten up to taking a course at 60 on 'the art of web design'. In

Ghana, the hierarchical system as we know it is in place. Children start Kindergarten at 4 or 5. From there, they go on to Primary school until the age of 11 or 12. Then, if they are lucky enough, it is off to Junior Secondary School (J.S.S). After 3 years of J.S.S, those with high enough grades go to Senior Secondary School (S.S.S). I was not sure where I would find myself working as it was up to the organisation in Accra to place us but I had it my mind that I would like to be in a J.S.S. J.S.S has children from the age of 11 to 15—in theory. I had a boy of 18 in my class and I am sure there were many more.

There are 7,122 Junior Secondary Schools in Ghana. 3,550 of them have toilets and water. There are 29,477 trained male teachers and 12,388 trained female teachers. Working (mainly in rural schools) teachers who are untrained number 10,929 men and 1,416 women. I had read that the system was improving in Ghana compared with its neighbouring countries but that they needed teachers. The villages are an undesirable location for trained teachers and very often, the very places that need the expertise are left with teachers who are untrained or were deemed unsatisfactory in their previous school. Having read this, the train of thought which drives our egos started to process in my mind. People were poor, lacked basic education. So I stepped up. Do I not want to be the hero going into the depths of despair? Would this not massage my ego? These illusions of grandeur had to be left behind and a journey of self discovery was going to be just as important as the acquisition of knowledge from the less developed world.

Months of questioning my reasons for doing this led me to a place of curiosity, a search for enlightenment by living my life with knowledge of how others lived theirs. This had to be the only reason. Living in Ireland, cruising along is fine, but surely I could live with more passion if my knowledge was greater and any small difference that I could make to either my own life or that of someone who appreciated it, would be significant. I wasn't to know what lay ahead or quite how changed my life would become. I was single, free and hungry for knowledge and experience at the ripe old age of 27.

Education was a field I was interested in and I had spent weeks reading about the educational background this first-to-be-liberated Sub-Saharan African country had. Its deep cultural roots, tribal customs and colourful diversity also whet my appetite for knowledge. What I would experience and what I read would certainly overlap but through my own openness and sheer interest, there would be moments which no words written could have prepared me for.

Ghana, being the first Sub-Saharan African nation to achieve independence has a complex educational background combining Christian missions, post-colonialism and Kwame Nkrumah's (Ghana's first President post independence who remains a controversial figure in their history) vision of a United Africa, which, like Nelson Mandela, was a quest for which he was prepared to die for.

In order to understand people in a nation, I always find it invaluable to be familiar with their historical background. This helps me in accepting behaviour and understanding why it is so. Take Ireland for example. Our obsession with owning property may look strange to a central European who is used to renting. But looking back in our history shows that our sense of oppression and being thrown off our own land makes our behaviour comprehendible. Indeed, looking backing at the Celts, Normans and Vikings could equally explain most people's temperaments.

This is why I needed to find out what kind of people I was dealing with.

Before these colonial times, Ghana was made up of 5 main groups whose names seemed impossible to pronounce or get my head around. If you do not find yourself in the native area/region of one of the groups, you would never know they exist, so I went to Ghana armed with all this over-the-top knowledge and rhymed off the groups—Akans, Mole-Dagbani, Guan, Ga-Adengbe and Ewe!

I was entering a world made up of ethnic groups, much like our own society in a way, but much more obvious when black skin is involved. I took the time to allow a sense of awareness to be triggered, then the characteristics of these ethnic groups are quite prevalent. I recognised that knowing something of the background certainly assists in understanding the people. This leads to a certain amount of generalisation throughout which I think, while not always welcome, is necessary to understand an idea.

I felt that a certain amount of stereotyping was acceptable in this case. I was a white, potato-eating, Irish-dancing Catholic and, as I engaged in the art of fine labelling, I discovered the man next to me on the plane was Akan. The Akans were the largest group in Ghana, he explained. As his intriguing rendition of Ghanaian tribal evolution continued, the plane passed over Europe and into North Africa. The Akan consists of 2 sub-groups—Twi and Fante speakers. I was going to stay in area where they spoke Twi. 'Oh great', I thought to myself, 'practically my second language'!

Needless to say, I was very happy and proud to have learned *Ete Sen* means 'How are you?' and *bera* (pronounced 'bra') which means 'come here'. I was wondering just how far these expressions would get me. At that time, it was a language I would never really need to learn. I had a tongue which half the world knew or wanted to learn so I was safe. It is amazing how people express themselves through language, so how can we really know how a people think without understanding their true expression?

Interpretation and translation will take us to an ostensible level of understanding. We can behave as language realists and agree that we know what people mean because we have it looked it up in a dictionary. But, far deeper than that, is the concept that a sentence can hold a lot more than the words that are in it. Language will be an issue later but just to give an example. The word for 'white person' in Twi is '*Obruni*'.

So, you are warned that you will hear this lot (and you really do need to be prepared. Many volunteers leave early as they can not handle the constant trail of the word 'obruni') and that it means you are white as oppose to their black skin. However, the meaning of the word is really 'person of the horizon'. It reflects the people they first saw coming towards Africa before the colonial times. It represents anyone from any country outside Africa, including Asians. So, the word symbolises, not only skin colour, but also that you are unknown to them. In Europe and other parts of the world, we tend to group people much more specifically so that we do know them because we have put a word on who they are. We do like to be clear when it comes to the grouping of people who are not the same as us.

Now that I speak a reasonable amount of Twi (to the best I can hope for given the pronunciation problems) I can tell you that learning it was no mean feat! The meaning of the words could not be translated and it is difficult to find one word to describe something similar to what I had been used to. I hope one day to have a better grip on this strange-sounding language.

The man next to me, I now knew, was a history teacher, so, luckily (or unluckily) he was in a position to give me a rundown on Ghanaian history which I will kindly share with my readers.

The Akan originated in the old Ghana Empire, he continued, which is presently covered by Mauritania, Senegal and Mali. They established the Bono Kingdom in the 13th Century and stayed together for 200 years before separating into various sub-groups. One of the Twi speaking Akan was the Asante. This particular group were what most people's image of Ghana would come from—the colourful cloth, Kente, the gold, the royalty and everything else that goes with a wealthy kingdom. I wondered why this nation was not rich but did not interrupt with my questions at this time. During the time of British rule, Ghana was known as the Gold Coast for its abundance of Gold and it was the Asante who profited mostly from a relationship with the British during this time. I did, however, interrupt at this point to find common ground and share in the historical plight of British colonialism but to no avail. Despite all that had happened, there was a respect and admiration for the British.

Although the Akan are the largest group in Ghana, there are also 4 others (which my neighbour neglected to inform me about).

Then there is the Mole-Dagbani who came from Chad. They descend from a warlike people led by Tohazie, much resembling the Irish who descended from Vikings. They are to be found in Northern Ghana. The descendants of Tohazie were said to be warlike and aggressive but I can see no evidence of this from their behaviour of today, but then I stayed clear of the topics of religion or politics.

The Guan group are the earliest inhabitants of Ghana. They came from what is now Burkina Faso. Guan speaking people live in the Northern, Eastern, Central and Volta regions. It is not known exactly where they came from but, again, it is said to be a region of Burkina Faso.

The Ga-Adangbe originated in Nigeria and came to settle in the capital, Accra. Lastly, there are the Ewe people who came from Togo and who were ruled by a very wicked king named Agorkorli. The movement of ethnic groups stemmed from a quest for fertile land and a search for water, trade, protection and a pure sense of adventure. The childrens' fairy tales in Ghana are mainly based on stories from these times.

Much like them, my sense of adventure was about to begin.

The flight stopped in Nigeria and then continued to Ghana, hitting a violent storm on the way in. It became apparent that the pilot should not have left Lagos given that the storm was in front. He seemed to think he could have avoided it. As the plane moved from side to side, I glanced to see my friend next to me praying as most Ghanaians do, especially when death is probable. These people believe that death is always close—giving them an intense lust for life. Most of our feelings are intensified by the idea that it will not be forever. We tend to stay away from the subject of our mortality. If we discuss it in a group of friends, we are seen to be 'morbid'! It is a pity really. Now that I do discuss my eminent passing, it feels so refreshing to be alive.

I chose to put my head into crash position as my faith then was not as strong as those around me.

The aeroplane finally landed a little off the runway and I wondered what I had done and why I had chosen to come alone. Some of the volunteers seem to travel together but there was nobody else from Dublin going to Ghana at that time so I shared my thoughts with myself.

The heat hit me when I stepped off the plane like a dry wave. The sweat started and the ground ahead looked drier than I had ever seen. I took a breath and walked out to meet a person sent by the organisation.

They were late. Something not foreign to the Ghanaians. I waited a long time and finally asked a taxi driver to lend me his phone for the grand total of €10.I would find out later just how duped I was. In the meantime, a huge fight broke out and all I could hear was shouting and screaming. What on earth was I doing here?

Eventually, they arrived! I saw this very tall, very black man approach with a massive smile across his face followed by a small man who looked like something out of an RnB video. They didn't seem to know who I was but I was easy to spot and so informed me they were my drivers. What can you do?

I got into the car and looked out the window at the Ghanaians going about their daily life.

I realised right at that moment that this was going to be just fine. It took me a few days to truly believe that. (maybe more)

I had arrived 4 days before I was suppose to it turned out. I was, therefore, brought to a hotel in the middle of Accra where I stayed completely by myself for 3 days. I had no idea what was happening. I was trying to order anything from the menu that I couls understand, usually rice and fish. It was absolutely delicious! I watched Nigerian films on the hotel T.V and ventured out the odd time to observe the Ghanaians way of life. It was actually nice to have had that 'lost' time where I got some thoughts together and swam out of it alive and happy!

It was organised that I would stay with a family in an Eastern region village. The journey there was interesting, to say the least and after 2 car changes (break-downs), I finally arrived. However, the man who was to host him was very ill and would not be able to take me in. I was taken to a different village, to a family who were 'happy to have me' and so, off we went. I knew I would need to find my own work there and so I would have to get to know the neighbours!

Despite the warmth of my new family, I cried myself to sleep in thee house for a few nights. Loneliness crept in through the door and I reminded myself that loneliness is not absence of people but absence of direction. Once I found my reasons and purpose, I would be fine. I was also greatly concerned by the fact that the toilet had no water!!

I had a lot of learning to do, both academic and self-exploration but I knew this was the place for it. A feeling of being at home, a new home hit me and I stopped being scared and started to live more than ever before, opening my eyes to the world and to myself.

As I ventured into this new world I couldn't help but think how a parallel may well be drawn between this African nation and the nation I had grown up in.

The imperialistic elements of colonialism, suppression, a quest for land and resources and oppression were not altogether far removed from the Ireland my ancestors had grown up in. Most people around the world are familiar with the epic history of their past. We learned in school how, just like the people who make up Ghana today arrived, we too had our groups who contribute to our culture today. Each of us has some ancient culture who stemmed from a Viking, Celt or Norman. And, just like Ghana, certain individuals believed the country to be resourceful and beautiful enough to merit a colonial quest.

In Ghana, the taste of this concept is still very much in their mouths. As mentioned before, there is no outright loathing of the British or even any unkind words to be said against them. They do not cheer for any other team but England or dwell in the pitiful state they found themselves in under British rule. On the contrary, they may have fought long and hard to become the first free African Nation but now most Ghanaians respect their former rulers as they respect other Europeans. They see them in many ways superior which, to me, is all the words of pain and bitterness wrapped in a different package.

In order to understand further the nature of these people, I had looked at their more recent history and how that legacy of rule has left the children in the school with this idea that they are inferior to their white counterparts. During a lesson of English grammar, I asked the children if they had any questions—only to be met by: 'Madame, please, why are you white people better at everything that you do and we can't make any progress here in Africa?' I was honestly not informed enough to pass any remark on this so I vowed to look back at their history and, for the moment, ask my student to keep his eye on the lesson. In some way, I feel this was an answer to the question-lying somewhere between a good education and a lack of understanding from all parties involved.

CHAPTER 2

A BRIEF HISTORY

It is always something of habit of mine to seek understanding of people through their history. We may say history is 'not our thing' or 'I never liked history' but the truth is that we can not be who we were suppose to be in the future if we don't know where we came from in the past. We Irish must know that especially. We are shaped in so many ways by the behaviour of our ancestors. We can already see in our children that they are being shaped by the present and technology will be valued more in their future than anything because we encourage them to embrace it. Imagine different aspects of the African past being embraced or indeed that of Europe. I will not make a case for colonialism in any way nor that for slavery but I can say by having an understanding of the culture embraced by Europeans in the past means I can accept the reason why they did what they did. It doesn't mean I like that but that's the most open way to look at anthropology (and perhaps the only way). White people in Europe and America back in the time of the slave trade saw themselves as superior because that is the way they were presented with the 'fact' by those who nurture them. There was no reason for them to question it. For generations, it was the truth to them and, so, those who acted upon it were not committing evil acts but following the next step in developing their world at the expense of 'barbarians'. It made complete sense to them; in fact, it would have been a sign of weakness to do nothing. In today's world, we continue this mentality but it is allowed to manifest in much more subtle way but serves the same purpose. We just need to look at China and Tibet or Israel and Palestine. Where there are those who show the power, there will be those who submit to it. If there is a superior, there must also be an inferior and how easy it is to convince people of this when they don't know any better.

The Portuguese were the first of these Europeans to arrive in Ghana in 1471. The Portuguese were unusual in their colonial methods and built relationships with the natives, negotiating with chiefs for land and seriously doing business. They had no desire to take the land from the people, pillage them or steal their resources. Their trading agreement worked in their favour and they benefited considerably by building forts in Cape Coast as a trading post. However, their buildings would be a haven for those who followed, and to be used in very different ways. It was the Dutch who scuppered the Portuguese plans when a conflict arose in the 16th century between Spain and Holland. Around 1642 was when the forts fell to the hands of the Dutch. The gold resources were very appealing to the Dutch but they also saw a great business in the buying and selling of slaves. Many people understand that this slavery was an awful heart wrenching experience for the African people. But it was not only the degradation of being a slave, or the rotten treatment and separation from their families that caused suffering. The continent would change from fairly humble ways of life to conflicts and rivalry. Weapons were brought in on the ships, giving local people a new method to solve their own, previously, minor conflicts. Tribes began to divide, communities were destroyed. Along with the Dutch, came the French, the Danish and the British. The British were particularly successful in the commercial aspect of the slave trade. However, the loss of American colonies in the 18th century saw a large decrease in the demand for slaves. The British looked to Africa to deal in raw materials with and discontinue the slave trade. Under pressure from humanitarians and industrialists, the British finally passed a law in 1807 which made slavery illegal. The Danes and Dutch pulled out around this time, leaving the British to control trading activities in and out of Ghana.

The road to independence was very interesting in Ghana. The people learned to protest against unfair British laws such as not allowing certain cultural practices, land rights and many others. A political system was beginning to grow and the people were gaining strength against their colonial counterparts. Eventually, under pressure, some schools were built which meant educated citizens and further revolt. Some administrative roles were given to local people when previously all such roles were appointed by the Crown. When World War II came along, the world saw an emergence of political parties and Ghana was not left behind on this. Dr Kwame Nkrumah led the CPP (Convention People's Party) into an election which they won. The British could finally see that the Ghanaian people were capable of governing themselves and finally bowed to pressure in 1957. Ghana became the first Sub-Saharan country to achieve independence.

This brief history may lead us to believe there remains this animosity between the Ghanaians and the British but, as I discovered from my plane journey over, I was surprised to see that this was not the case. Being familiar with my own history, there has always been a tension with Ireland's previous colonial power (even if it is only another way to identify ourselves) but here people respected the British, took an interest in the Royal family, strived to make it to London to meet them. It was wonderfully refreshing to see that they forgave the suffering of the past, and in fact, saw that the trade agreement helped the country to find its feet. They do not talk of the slave trade but certainly other resources which they feel they didn't have the knowledge to exploit previously. They believe their link with Britain opened them up to the world. They are not a people to hold grudges anyway and they seem not to have a problem with any particular nation, even in their own continent. Some characteristics of the culture may be linked to their past and one I observed most profoundly was their willingness to submit to authority. It shows great respect but it can sometimes be to people's detriment. There was a young man who lived near me in the village whose mother had stayed in a smaller village and he had come to try to make money. He lived with a family and the man in this family treated him like a slave. He was so unhappy, so one day I suggested he stand up to him and tell him he is tired and he would do the work later. He was surprised at my lack of understanding in the situation and felt I was asking him to disrespect in some way. This is such a no—go area in Ghana and perhaps it is something that lingers from historical happenings. I certainly learned a lesson form it and reminded myself to remain as an observer as much as possible.

Post independence was also an interesting experience for Ghanaian people and there seems to be a division on the benefits of Kwame Nkrumah's political agenda. Some have a picture of him on their wall beside Jesus and Mandela. Others think he stole from the country creating his own wealth and forgetting what he was originally standing for. There was plenty of money in their post-colonial budget, I am told, but not enough was done with the country. There are those who say Independence was more important and freedom can never be bought. I remain divided.

CHAPTER 3

A SYSTEM OF LEARNING

I befriended the man downstairs from where I was living who happened to be the principal of the local J.S.S. I remembered my father always told me that it wasn't what you know but who you know and I have always found people to be the most useful in moving ahead in life. Mr. Achaempong was a strict looking man and when I first saw him, I felt like running the other way. However, when I got to know him, we had a wonderful relationship and he was very kind in setting me up in the school as a teacher. I would teach French and English to a class in first year, second year and third year.

The education system in Ghana is one which is constantly improving and, in relation to its neighbouring French-Speaking countries, it is thriving. The theoretical approach to the new system developed in 1996 is based on a system which is destined to create an environment free from discrimination associated with your sex or academic ability. The system is called FCUBE—Free Compulsory Basic education Programme. This means that the government must provide a high standard of education if they want to see their budgets continued. It relates to teaching standards, empowering everybody to attend and improving management within the education sector.

From my own experience, there is definitely a drive for a better system in Ghana. There are certain factors which will inhibit this progress but at least it is improving. The first issue is teacher's pay. Many teachers are paid very little but the other issue is that a teacher can begin a teaching job in Ghana and have to wait 1 year for their pay. Reasons

19

are given such as induction service, processing of papers but ultimately it leaves families struggling and building significant debt. The other issue I looked at was the idea that certain villages were assigned teachers who were not 'suitable' for other schools and quite often this meant that they did not have an ability to teach but sending them to a village school would solve the problem. Many of the village schools operate at sub standard quality but some of them are fantastic. In the school I was in I saw dedicated teachers and a high number of children attending. The classroom population unfortunately does not allow for weaker students to thrive and this is sad thing to watch.

Paul Nkwi, who is an anthropologist from Cameroon, said that at independence, each African nation created its own institute of higher learning based on European Universities. He goes on to say there was little attention paid to African culture.

The number of schools in Ghana has grown considerably which is a great thing and contributes greatly to their economic progress. In a population of around 24 million, there are 7,122 J.S.S. However, 3,550 of them have no toilet facilities. There are 29,477 trained male teachers and 12,388 female teachers but there are also 10,929 untrained male teachers and 1,416 untrained female teachers. The National Board for professional Technical Examinations is responsible for testing the students and their statistics give an insight into the progress of the Ghanaian students. Of the 5.1 million students attending schools in Ghana, only about 34% gain access to universities. There are now 68% of the population at primary school, 23% at J.S.S and only 10% going on to S.S.S.

From my first few days there, I thought every child was at the school. The class rooms were packed and the streets were full of this bright blue coloured uniform. I then started to notice the amount of children working and serving those in uniforms their rice and fruit. Quite a contrast on the streets of Akim Oda (my new village).

Quite often by the time students are ready to move to senior secondary school, the money in the family has run out, or there is another child who needs to be sent to school and the parents can't pay the fee for all of them. Other times, they are forced to work for economic reasons or, if they are weak, they may not have the encouragement to move on to the next step. There are no resources there to assist them.

I was staying in a house which was in the centre of a large community. The 2 boys downstairs were so eager to go to school everyday and thought themselves so lucky that they had the opportunity. I had taken it for granted at home that everyone goes to school and complains at that! Their mother was working in another city and sent their school fees home so they could start S.S.S which was where they were.

Within the education system in Ghana in there is great degree of what is described as 'depositing'. This idea comes from the Brazilian educator and philosopher, Paolo Friere who wrote extensively on education for the native people and how it should move away from colonial pedagogy and be more localised. The teacher is quite often an authoritarian figure who expects students to listen and memorise correct answers rather than think about it themselves and construct the knowledge. Like depositing money in a bank, you are depositing information through mainly drilling methods and taking it out on demand. There is not much space for allowing students to develop thought. It would have been quite similar in Ireland in the past where people were made to memorise exercises. It is now we can see a negative attitude to certain subjects such as Irish and maths because the teacher never made the subjects come alive, there was no connection with reality. It was just about having an ability to memorise something and if you couldn't due to some learning difficulty or personal issue, you were considered stupid and sent away. If we look to Asian cultures, the students are thought how to solve problems and cognitively approach

21

everyday tasks. This is very different in Ghanaian teaching. Students could say the verb 'to do' a hundred times, get it correct in a test but most of them then say 'he don't have money' straight after.

I spoke to the principal of the school in the first few days about the education system but I felt my questions were offending him in some way or how he ran the school so I had to go back to the books for some more information. I spent the first week working and reading until I found no further use for the words on the pages and got to know the reality.

The first call for a university for West Africa came from three 19th century black intellectuals: Dr. James Africanus Beale Horton (1835-1883), Edward Blyden (1832-1912), and Rev. James Johnson (1839-1917). Blyden, for example, called for an indigenous university that would "release Africa from the grip of the despotic mind and restore cultural self-respect among Africans" and Johnson called for "an institution that would leave undisturbed our peculiarities"

Kwame Nkrumah wanted to push for education through African culture. He felt people would be better educated if they knew their own culture better. It is a difficult one to decide. Are they better with their own curriculum or do they take material from other countries?

A century later, while opening the Institute of African Studies at the University of Ghana-Legon, Dr. Kwame Nkrumah invited African scholars to study Africa in all of its complexities and diversity, in order to stimulate respect for the idea of African unity. The study of African cultures and people was not to be limited to conventional and regional boundaries. Nkrumah urged that all investigations "must inevitably lead towards the exploration of the connections between musical forms, the dances, the literature, the plastic arts, the philosophical and religious beliefs, the systems of government, the patterns of trade and economic organization that have been developed here in Ghana and in the cultures of other African peoples and other regions of Africa" In his book

Africa Must Unite (Nkrumah 1963), culture is also a dominant theme. Anthropological studies would be part of the essential programs of the Institute. It is difficult to see whether this has been implemented. For most people, even their local language, which is taught in the schools, is relatively unknown in the written form.

Despite the problems mentioned above, the school system works for many people in Ghana. If you have enough to pay the school fees, are close to the school and work hard, the future is very bright for many students. I was now going to meet these students and see for myself how the system worked here.

CHAPTER 4

EYES OFF THE GAME

The task that was to be my mission in Ghana boiled over into something much more controversial. As I settled into researching the education system, writing notes and studying this population, I started to make friends. Just in any other everyday situation, I would wake up in the morning and get on with the day ahead.

A typical day started at 6.00am. This was a time I had never seen either side of but in the middle of an African village, it is a release to get up and escape the sounds that surround you. The sounds of the women brushing relentlessly outside, stooped low down for hours on end cleaning up from yesterdays' daily events. The sounds of the cars that beep all the time looking for fares or warning people they are coming. This is due to the fact that the roads are not built for humans and traffic. There are no paths and the sewage runs along the side of the road, so that you are confronted with falling into a river of decrement or landing on the bonnet of a car. There are, of course, the sounds of the cars themselves, the engines roaring in vehicles that wouldn't be allowed on roads in other parts of the world and where bribing mechanics and car testers is a no go area!! The cars have been sent from Europe to Ghana having been scrapped and deemed worthless by Western standards. Yet, the Ghanaians will use every resource necessary and get that car working even if it means breaking down every few hundred miles! I have often been in a taxi travelling from one village to another when the driver kindly asks if I would step out and push. I have rolled back down a hill with a horrified driver concerned that the 'white lady' must be terrified.

Terror was not an emotion I was feeling at these moments. If not dangerous, they are often extremely funny situations to be part of. It feels like you are part of an episode of the Flintstones!

It is amazing how so many onlookers will rally around where there is no chance of road-side assistance from an insurance company. Many an African village has been established through concern over a certain issue. People gather to see what has happened and suddenly these people need a place to sit, to sleep, to eat. This becomes a place where the community gather, employment is created and therein lies a beautiful community-based village lacking in prominence but as rich in spirit as any other African settlement.

The final and most profound sound of all is the one species that is of great importance to the people of this village—the Cockerel! Even though the noise would wake me up, I forgave the animal for providing a high level of entertainment in the village. There would often be discussions about this animal—how many people own, how big they are and if certain men had bigger ones than others. Without going into too much detail, I am sure it is clear that, while completely immature on my part, the shortened version of this animal's name in the midst of these debates did entice the odd giggle from me.

So, with all the wonderful sounds of the African morning, I would rise up to fulfil my duties as a guest in my family's house.

In the morning, it was appropriate to read the scriptures with my family. They were Jehovah's Witnesses and, as I was part of their home, I became part of their millenarian circle. It was the most enhancing experience of my life. I may not have agreed with everything that was said but their own discipline in their faith is inspiring. An epiphany emerged over the course of my time there. I questioned other religions and whether I had to always respect their beliefs. It stands that, we do not have to always like other peoples' practices, beliefs or customs but it is certainly more rewarding to respect them and to find a way to understand them. When a belief system stems into something which fails to recognise human rights, I believe, it is then that we can stand up and say we do not accept it. This would be in extreme cases of genital mutilation or suppression of rights (usually women). In these cases there is no anthropological argument. Perhaps we should recognise a standard set of moral rights and live by them. However, if a group of people do not recognise Christmas or birthdays, who am I to judge? Does my faith hold so much weight in the grand scale of the world that I can safely say I know best? The answer was 'no' and so I sat and listened intently, learning what I could from reading passages that can mean so much. I had never picked up the Bible willingly in my life and only knew readings from Sunday mass. ('knew' is bit of an exaggeration as they were never explained to me). Here, I was studying its very core and understanding was suddenly within reach. The parables, while they take them to be literal and I took them to be symbolic, spoke of everything that exists in our daily life. There was no point in being cynical as it felt as if the stories were written for myself and everyone I knew. I became connected with characters, entrenched in beautiful descriptions and obsessed with the moral teachings represented in the Gospels. I did not become, what our society would deem 'holy Joe' over night, but I did enjoy, and still do, the teachings of the Bible if we take them as they mean to be taken. Looking at my host family during our Bible study mornings and at many other Africans, I saw an underlying difference between them and the Western world. Many in Ghana believe God will save them so it is not worth worrying over what leaves little space for what we would deem 'progression'. On the contrary, many Westerners believe what we do has no connection to God therefore we are out for ourselves. Would a place in the middle not be a much better way to look at the world? In my host household I was introduced to this concept of pure belief in something/somebody and a love for Jesus that I never knew possible. This love, whether we believe in Him or not, is so magical that the mere existence of it allows you not to get overshadowed by the fact that there may well be a fictional character involved.

In my own knowledge of Jehovah Witnessing, I always understood that they kept themselves apart from others. They have somewhat of a negative reputation in most parts of the world for being overpowering and dominant in their preaching. However, these people only wanted to share a knowledge that they truly believed to contribute to salvation with whomever they met. It was inspiring to see such discipline and pure faith in a system that helps them to survive any adversity that may come along. Whatever we may think about faith or religion, I think we could agree that if it helps people cope in difficult times and allows them to lead a contented life, we would not begrudge that.

These mornings spent with the family empowered me to accept people and analyse where my ego stopped in this country and where my understanding began. Only with this in mind could I have allowed myself to really open up to the things that were going to happen and the decisions I would have to make.

After scripture reading, I would have breakfast. The Ghanaians eat what they call 'heavy food' for breakfast and laughed at the mere idea that I might join them. Much to their surprise and detriment to my stomach I partook in dining on fish, eggs, rich with spicy sauce and banku at 6.30 in the morning. Banku is made from cornmeal (maize), which has been grinded into powder and has water added to it to make it like a stodgy lump of mashed potato. I never really got used to the taste of it although I love Ghanaian food. It has an unusual texture and sour aftertaste. It is usually served with a spicy sauce or stew (which Ghanaians call 'soup'). There were mornings where I simply could not face such a feast and stuck to my coffee, porridge and bread. They were always more comfortable when I stuck to the menu of my 'homeland' as it was not an uncommon event to see the white volunteers extremely ill during their time in Ghana.

After breakfast (or sometimes before) it was time for a shower. It was a great awakening! At the beginning of my new found African life, the water situation proved to be a difficult challenge. As it was not in abundance, one had to plan their usage before entering the bathroom. If a certain breakfast had caused gastric issues, it was best to leave the hair unwashed and concentrate on the amount needed to flush the toilet! However, mostly, there was enough to go around as, in this particular place, the water ran in the taps at certain times. The bathroom was just a few tiles on the floor and the whole room was full of buckets. When the water flow comes to the village, all of those buckets must be filled as it could be a long time before it happened again. A cold bucket of water was meticulously poured over a sweating head. I took great care in the amount of water I used, unlike my behaviour in Ireland. The same water I used to wash my hair would be what I used for the body. I had never felt cleaner!

Away from Ghana, cold showers were what I missed most. It was the best way to wake up and knowing how hot you would be, it was so refreshing.

It was then time to go to work in the Junior Secondary School in the village.

The first day I started was one of the most profound learning experiences of my life. A classroom of 70 children and a teacher very much lacking in disciplinary experience!

As soon as I walked into my English class, I knew there was a sense of novelty for the children and my white face approaching nervously, hand empty of cane, sweat dripping and flip flops made my presence comic to them. The principal left me to it aware that I had a teaching certificate, years of experience and enthusiasm running through my veins. However, this moment made me feel so exposed and vulnerable. A fish out of water. There was only one thing for it. I had to regain the power. I had to lay down a law from the first minute. If not, I may as

29

well take my place on the concrete floor and call them one by one to walk on my emaciated body.

So, I watched them for 1 minute talk and laugh as I began a lesson on 'reading text for understanding' and then the nerves and fear turned to anger and action. I had not prepared my class as I had no idea prior to this moment who or what I would be teaching. This lack of preparation was written all over my face as any teacher will be well aware of. As the noise levels began to rise, I threw my books on the desk and in my most stern voice I said 'I have come a long way to give my time to teaching you and this is how you decide to treat me'. I then sauntered out the door across the school sport's ground. I was beginning to feel despair creeping into my bones, (I had no intention of giving up) when two sweet children came to me and said 'Madame, we are so sorry. We promise to listen to you and be quiet. Please come back'. Thank God they hadn't called my bluff. My mother would have been proud of my poker face!

So I accepted their apology and their promise and walked back to the class with my head held high and the power back in my hands. It is the only way to teach such a huge group. The maximum I had had in a class of adults learning English was 14! I complained to the director about that at the time because I couldn't give enough attention to the students. This was a whole other ball game.

As a great fan of Paulo Freire, I wanted to follow some of his basic concepts relating to education of people who have previously been oppressed. Of course, not these particular children but those in their history. These children had been exposed to what he refers to as 'depositing' information within the analogy of banking. Repetition is used in order to learn and the teacher imparts knowledge on them which they must remember for the purpose of remembering.

An article published in 'Comparative Education' in 2006 set out to report on the education system of Ghana with a vision in mind of successful schooling. In its introduction, it states:

'Discourse analysis of classroom teaching and learning in sub-Saharan Africa generally shows the African teacher as an authoritarian classroom figurehead who expects students to listen and memorize correct answers or procedures rather than construct knowledge themselves'

I was not here to change anything within the system (not that I could) or, indeed, to criticise it any way but I did want the children in my class to become part of what they were learning. To see themselves as examples of what was being taught. If I could appeal to them personally and to their culture, the information would be relevant to them and would increase their ability to retain it. I wasn't sure if I was doing the right thing by introducing them to something different when they were so used to a certain method. The truth was—I didn't know any other way to teach. I had come only armed with a TEFL certificate and experience in dealing with obedient adults! The school had accepted me in this school knowing that I had come from a different system and they were willing to allow the children to participate in a new way of learning. They had never had a volunteer at the school either so it was strange to all of us.

When we did plays from the text books, I would ask them to take on character roles and act out the play, learning new grammar structures and vocabulary while recognising that education does not have to be fragmented. They themselves are characters in the world; they do have roles to play. In these contexts, they can use the language learned in class. It all becomes relevant to them.

For grammar, they would have to come up with their own examples. This was a particularly challenging task. It backfired on me in so many cases when mountains of homework to correct made no sense. There was a lack of imagination among many of them as they just expected to repeat everything and not to have to imagine an everyday situation. This could also be said of the Irish education system and perhaps others around the world where exam-based curriculum is regurgitated knowledge on paper.

Day by day, they adapted to my methods and I learned how they received new information. (I was genuinely learning as much as them). Most of the time, it worked well. There were so many problems, it has to be said. I spent a lot of time between classes observing what was going on around me. Big classes, sharing books and desks and the lack of facilities all made the physical environment difficult to work in. With no extra resources, children who were weaker got left behind and they were usually the ones who got beaten the most. It was a vicious circle. The more they got wrong, the more they got punished and the more likely they were to be left behind—broken and dishevelled after their experience. The students who were smart and ambitious rarely got punished and moved way ahead of others. Some children always copied from their friends which was not something that bothered other teachers. 'As long as the work was done' seemed to be the general consensus. All of the work was usually the same so it wasn't noticeable anyway. If students are repeating what you say, why would you question if all the exercises are the same?

I was very strict on that. If I found out that people had copied, I would move them to a place which was isolated. Usually it meant them getting a beating when they were found out so I hated doing it. I was in control of the punishment so it was all very difficult to know what to do. If someone did get into trouble in my class, another teacher would come in and carry out the punishment making me sit back feeling sad and guilty. Most of the staff there were very loving to the children and the atmosphere was wonderful overall. It was just these moments that sent shivers down my spine. I asked once if I could deal with a particular student and it was met with disdain and offence so I never questioned it again. It was so difficult to find that balance between remaining objective and speaking up.

It was important to find what appealed to my kids. Teaching French to the first years was no mean feat but as soon as I recognised their love for music, we began classes by singing French songs. I didn't know French songs, to be perfectly honest, so I took English songs and changed the words! I began the first with a few verses of 'In the Jungle' from The Lion King, which went something like 'dans la jungle, la terrible jungle, le lion, il dort ce soir'! This was followed by a lot of 'a womba wa a womba wa' and laughter. I had won this class over too! Whatever it takes!

It was very enjoyable but the workload soon became overwhelming. I had 5 classes, teaching them English and French. The amount of copies to be corrected and tests to be prepared and marked soon got too much. I tried to share the workload and I did receive some help. I loved it so much that I got on with it, but I would sleep so early every night in preparation for the days that lay ahead.

The day went fast—clouded over with intense heat creating streams of perspiration which incessantly fell form my brow and every other part of the body. It was coming from places I never thought possible! As the school had no air conditioning or means of cooling down we all suffered our fate with cloth handkerchiefs and an abundance of pure water!

Lunch time came at around 12.00 and, being a westerner, I was always given fruit to eat as my family did not want to subject me to the 'heavy food' of the locals. However, at that stage in the day, hunger roared through my body and fruit was not going to cut it. The children went to get me fish and yam most days with this incredibly spicy sauce to accompany it. Wonderful. As the days went on, it all became so normal so quickly. The human being's ability to adapt never ceased to amaze me.

As the days passed, my workload became greater and greater. The school had no French teacher as he had 'run away' just before I arrived. The students had exams in this subject so they needed some guidance. As a result, I was now teaching French to first years and I had 4 different English classes. When there are 65 to 70 children in a class, correcting essays and questions is no mean feat (as a third level tutor now, I still complain about that very thing!). I was also asked by the head teacher to create some mock exams for the finals so that was another major project.

The last class of English in the afternoon was a sweat fest for both me and the children.

The sun was high and it scorched, rendering us incapable of any physical activity or major inspiration. People talk of the heat in Africa slowing the people down. It is certainly a factor which plays a part in cessation of productivity. Incessant heat without a breeze makes concentration extremely difficult. There are no air-conditioning facilities and fans are few and far between. Most of the schools are partly outdoors so it is a case of sticking it out and drinking as much water as possible.

I always had a sense of paranoia in my country when the issue of perspiration came up. Sweaty armpits in front of other people, beads on the forehead on that first date, underwear sticking to us and so the thought of a romance leading anywhere was cringe worthy. However, here, where sweating was a natural defence against the heat (as it is everywhere) I found myself becoming comfortable with the fluid that drained from every orifice in my body. The handkerchief I carried became very precious to me so that I would be able to see what I was doing and to fan myself when the time came to dance (which it did very often).

So, in the midst of the heat, at around 3 o'clock, the time came to walk home.

There was always someone around who wished to accompany me on my journey home which was gallant and, at the beginning, the security it provided was very welcome. However, my eyes had moved to something else. It was like that part in a science fiction film, where the camera zooms in on a vision which a character is encapsulated on. I had seen him. I knew where he worked. My eyes were no longer only fixed on the work I was here to do. I had now something of a distraction. My eyes were off the game.

CHAPTER 5

THE MEETING

In any culture, there is one occasion that gets everybody excited and brings families and friends together. The joining of two people in the eyes of God. Nowhere is it as celebrated as in Western Africa. The entire community gathers to help with the preparation. Women are out at 5am starting the fires, bringing the meat, the fufu is pounded (This is a meticulous job which involves a male using a very large stick to beat down on cassava and plantain while a female continuously adds water until it turns to a dough like substance. It is impressive as often the wooden stick will miss the woman's hand by a centimetre), the banku is stirred and the African fashionistas start to come out in their droves. The preparation is so wonderfully shared (financially also which really helps).

I was invited to this wedding on this day, one month after my arrival in Ghana. It was a friend of my host family and I had no idea who the couple were. My host mother wanted to bring me to show them she had a white girl staying with her and I was honoured to accompany her and to experience my first Ghanaian wedding. Having me staying with her was something of a status symbol apparently.

Coming from Ireland, where weddings are a fantastic excuse to get very drunk and make a show of ourselves (only speaking from experience), the Ghanaian wedding appeared much more civilised to me. The traditional element is very interesting but it concerns the parents a lot more than the bride and groom. In looking at the background of the engagement, the reason for this practice becomes clear.

In Ghana, one does not just simply begin a relationship, get to know each other and finally decide to marry. If a boy meets a girl and wishes to pursue her, until the issue of marriage is mentioned, it can be very difficult. The relationship is very often carried out without the parent's consent. Only when you are sure that you want to marry do you introduce your future spouse to a parent. It is unusual to see what we would call 'casual relationships' there. It more than likely has to be going somewhere.

Often, when a Ghanaian man meets a woman, he will say 'I love you' or 'I want to marry you' before a phone number is even exchanged! It can be quite a shock to hear this in the first 10 minutes but it is to ensure that the relationship is going to be genuine. In Twi, there are no adverbs. This means when men tell you they like you, there is no distinction between how they feel about you and the man on the street. They don't have 'really' or 'truly' or 'so much' which results in a loose violation of the word 'love'. All cultures and people are responsible for the abuse of this word so it is of no surprise to us.

The parents then decide if this person is right for their child and on this condition, the wedding goes ahead. It is often very much based on economic status. A friend of mine in Ghana has been in a relationship with his girlfriend for 12 years but, because of his low income and lack of prospects, it is very difficult for him to propose to her and get her parents consent.

On the day of the wedding, before the church, everyone meets at the bride's parents' house. The traditional wedding is very prominent in Ghana, but like many places, there are less and less of these kind of ceremonies and more emphasis on Western style weddings. At the bride's house, the groom's mother hands over gifts of Schnapps as a payment for the wife. During the speeches and exchange of gifts, the couple are often not present. I had no idea what was happening at that time and, despite having no idea of the dialogue exchanged, I cried at the mere sentiment of the ritual.

After this has taken place, the couple emerge and exchange vows. Then everyone changes and goes to the church. The general vows take place, followed by the most extravagant display of music and dancing. There is more dancing in the church than any wedding reception I have ever been to. It is time for the families to come together and it is a very hot, tiring and exhilarating experience. I thought this would be the closest I would come to such an extraordinary ritual.

The reception is a short affair involving some interesting customs. This part varies from wedding to wedding but is still very common in the villages. The couple stand near a display of balloons and the guests are invited to give the couple 1 Ghana Cedi each, which is about 80cent of a Euro and then burst a balloon (orange for the man and white for the woman in this case).

Certain people then seemed to be invited to the back to enjoy the alcohol on offer. I think the amount of money you offer can determine your V.I.P status as most people were left with the minerals at the front of house. There is also fufu out the back which I bee lined for as I was starving. The alcohol I avoided as I felt women were not really seen drinking so I stuck to malt. It took me some time to be comfortable with the fact that I was not drinking alcohol at such a lively wedding. I realised how much I took my own rituals for granted. As soon as I let go of the desire, I really enjoyed my soft drink and began to unwind.

Dancing then takes over as always.

That was the first time that I was to be the greatest entertainment for my hosts. Everyone thought my dancing method was so funny and laughed at me until they cried. I had to choose there and then whether to be shy and offended by this burst of mockery or take it in my stride. The latter is always much easier. I indulged them by moving my bum in true African style sticking it out as far as I could and wobbling my chest at the same time. This was even funnier as they pointed out that my bum was far too small for these moves and they didn't even venture a slag on the size of my chest! The women in my midst were larger than life ladies beautiful with their large feminine bodies proud to flaunt them to the crowd. I laughed along with them and danced twice as hard until they began copying my moves. It was then my turn to laugh at them and they appreciated my co-operation. It was a time in my life I will never forget. It is those little moments that last in life. The memories we create by behaving a certain way at a certain time. When we are the minority in a group, we have to trust that the majority know what they are doing and accept it. I was beginning to learn and I loved it.

At some point in all of the dancing, I took a break and stood by a wall observing the colourful African moves.

A man introduced himself to me and then to all of his friends. I really only noticed one in particular. He was the only one who didn't seem impressed by a white woman trying to fit in. His standoffish behaviour captured me. I wanted to know more. I asked him a question and he responded in broken English that he didn't speak English. He had heard I was an English teacher and asked me if I would be interested in giving him some classes. For some reason I was intrigued and agreed. At this point, nothing in this new world of mine phased me!

The wedding ended and I returned home sober and enlightened.

The following day was a Sunday and I sat preparing classes for the coming week.

There was a knock on my door and when I went to open it, there stood the so called 'student'. It turned out his English was perfect and he was also intrigued by me so he thought of the best way to get to see me again. Smart. Somewhat deceiving but smart. From that very moment, I could see flashes of changes and difficulties ahead but I didn't let them take over. After all, it was just going to be a friendship if anything. Why worry? Would I not return to my country and meet my prince charming?

I was brought back to my first week in Accra when I was given an 'orientation' with all the other volunteers before we were brought to our families. I had almost a week with young people from all over Europe, mainly Germany and Belgium. I was the only Irish there and by far the oldest! During this week, we had been given lessons on what to expect, some Twi phrases, advice on medicine, health and lots of other issues. The one thing that stood out was the advice given on Ghanaian men to the females of the group. At the time I listened carefully to what the liaison officer was saying and genuinely believed I would take her advice. She told us that is ok to make friends but stay clear of any advances, avoid intimate relationships and be very careful of the men in general. She was only concerned for our welfare and she was right in a way but I see now how volunteers could walk into their new temporary world more closed-minded that they probably should.

The days passed and then the moments came when I no longer wanted anyone to walk me home from school. I knew he worked nearby and I found myself passing by his part of the busy market on my way home. I made excuses that I wanted to be by myself, but lurking, in the noisy market place of the village was a man I knew I was addicted to.

At that time, I didn't really understand how love worked nor did I know the true workings of a relationship. I had been in relationships before but the fact that I was still single and in Ghana alone is proof they didn't work out too well. I believed at that time that there was one person for all of us. That we had to search for this person and, when we found them, we would live happily ever after. Whether it was down to the fairytales you are read as a child or the media exposure along with relentless reporting on the lifestyle of the rich and famous I don't know. Whatever the case, the conditioning of this ideal love, romantic love, meant I, like many of my clan, were victims of a culture. So, back then I made no decision about my feelings for him, I made no decisions about the future or about anything. Decisions were too tough. They meant consequences and, mostly, they meant hard work defending that which you thought you had decided upon.

But something had sparked in me, something that had never happened before. Apart from the attraction and love I felt for this man already, there was something much more anthropologically challenging going on. I needed to break down conditioned cultural barriers if I was to engage in this 'friendship'.

The first issue was one which I never thought would come up in me. I thought by my deciding to come to Ghana, I had made a statement to the world that I was definitely not racist. I had come to share the joy of the people of Africa! It takes an intimate relationship with a member of a different race to question your sense of what is real. Do we really get opportunities to question how we feel about the world?

I found myself mulling over all the issues raised by those I had ultimately criticised in my 'Intercultural past'. My coming to Ghana did not reflect an indelible level of tolerance. My journey was probably more of a justification of a life considered to be somewhat futile in my world.

Now, it was time to explore how I really felt and, while racism is a harsh word to use, it truly expresses the ignorance that lies beneath. The idea allows us to set ourselves apart from others outside our own familiar race and so, allow us to nestle happily into our comfort zone.

After our first month together, I was invited to my new 'friend's' birthday celebration in a local bar ('spot' as they are called there). It was the time to meet all the friends and allow myself to be judged as a potential girlfriend of this very popular 'big man' in town. The evening involved a few Ghanaian strong beers, a lot of laughter, many moments of confusion turned frustration trying to decipher the Twi and Pidgin English. That feeling that all aliens get when they are in this situation came over me. You feel stupid and 'shy' even though that is no reflection of your personality. I sat there quiet as a mouse while they were putting the world to right just because I didn't speak the same language. I tried my best to make a contribution and eventually they decided to speak English.

It was also the evening that this new relationship passed from friendship to intimacy, sealed by the most wonderful kiss a person can receive. His lips were large and soft and I could have stayed in that embrace forever. I left him that evening feeling like a light had sparked inside of me.

The following day came and those thoughts of ignorance started to occupy an otherwise content mind. I found myself projecting into the future and asking questions laced with traces of racism. He is black. How can I return home and say that I am in love with an African? What would people think—that I was too undesirable to find a man of my own race? I started to consider the reason for slavery, whether white consider themselves superior and if so, why. How would we ever be equal if we were to live in Europe? I surprised myself with these thoughts but I had to allow the thoughts to be released, to alter my metaphysics in some manner, think outside the box, so to speak. I knew deep down. In theory. I knew these things were not really important and that a human being has no ground to judge another on colour or any other factor. This realisation may be there but time has to be taken to get there. If we believe that we all know and practice the right way, we will be grossly mistaken when it comes to the big decisions. I had to know if I could break this barrier in front of me as high as a skyscraper and whether I had the ability to see past the colour of this man's skin. I also had to find out, more importantly, if I could see past the colour of my own skin. That frightened me. While I judged him, I was judging myself, believing I was defined by my whiteness if I was willing to define him by his blackness. If I could see deep into myself, then I had the ability to see deep into him. On our journey in life of self-discovery or whatever it may be, how often do we ponder our own skin colour? Very rarely, I would say. It is probably not necessary in most peoples' lives. So why, in order to discover another, would we then focus on theirs. Hypocritical reactions are expected but need to be curbed. It took time, but slowly I peeled back the layers of skin, and I found a warm loving person who didn't have to be defined by anything.

The second issue I found myself facing (and somewhat associated with the first) was related to the world of finance and economics. Even though he worked hard, everyday was a mission to have enough for the 3 daily meals and I had so much more than he had, even if that was very little in comparison to some of my fellow countrymen. Again, I started asking a major question. What was it that money meant to me? Did I see him as economically inferior or did I see how brave and determined he is to always find money for the important things in life that we took for granted? I didn't even realise at the time but all of these thoughts were leading to a place that I never thought I would find myself in.

Then there was the issue of education. Coming from a background of academia, I found myself wondering if I could ever be with someone less educated than I was. It amazes me at the time to even have this question enter my head but I think people sometimes need a platform to place their thoughts on and thrash them out. I knew I had a few letters after my name but did that mean that I was more intelligent or knowledgeable? He was to me, and all who knew him, a man of the world. He could discuss any topic with passion and enthusiasm. His understanding of human nature was impeccable and, as Oscar Wilde said: 'Nothing worth learning can ever be taught'. I would never take away from the fact that I am grateful for my qualifications, but he was also grateful for his, even if they came from the University of Life.

Then there were more practical issues to ponder over, giving me more excuses to run from this and retreat to the safety of the known. There was the distance for one. It would be too difficult to maintain a relationship from different continents. And whether the proverbial conflict of 'absence makes the heart grow fonder' or 'out of sight-out of mind' applied, there would always be a world between us. It is hard enough for people from North Dublin to sustain a relationship with someone from the South and here I am trying to imagine my phone bills and nights of loneliness. Could we make this work?

If we are focused on the end result, we can always get through the tough times; a philosophy spoken many times by my Ghanaian 'friend'. This came to be a very important to me when getting through difficult times.

Then there was the question of a visa. This, to be said, was a major question for me. All the stories of African men seeking women for visas, for their escape out of a land of poverty and suppression, they were all ringing through my head like loud bells deafening my reasoning and focus on the ever important feeling of love. It came and went all the time from my mind. The conflict in my mind was mounting. What did he really want from me? Ghana was not a land of poverty and suppression. People were poor, but happy and had enough to eat. Emmanuel Bombande, executive director of the West Africa Network for Peace building says that 'Ghana is a durable democracy which transmits to the region of West Africa.' There is hope that Ghana is the way through which the region may prosper and other nations look to it as an example.

This land is beautiful and he is proud of his country. There is no danger of persecution or war. Of course, there is always hope that there would be an easier way of life on far away hills but my new found love was not in any major hurry to seek the riches of a post 'Celtic Tiger' Ireland!. He had an opportunity to leave and that was pending. It was to the United States, but suddenly, with my presence and charming Irish eyes, he soon shifted his sights on a much smaller, greener and wetter land!

Eventually I let go of the feeling that I was being used for immigration status. My mind began to focus on the quest for legal recognition if we were ever to live as a couple in Ireland, though thus wasn't a real prospect.

Acquiring a visa for him to enter Ireland would be very difficult and I thought about the trouble that would bring.

One other issue which I thought little of at the time but which grew as soon as my family joined my journey was his religion. Catholic versus Protestant. This was a legacy I grew up thinking was a no go area and now it was suddenly in front of me. For other nationalities, this may not pose any problems but for the Irish it can be a major bone of contention. In Ghana, religious dominations are of little importance. This is not always the case across the African continent. Nigeria has always had confrontational issues between Christians and Muslims as have Sudan, who eventually decided to separate as a result. Ghana is very refreshing in this way.

The real relevance comes through the fact that you are Christian. If you happen to be of the Islam faith, Jewish or anything else, you are embraced as having some affiliation with God, whatever you may call him. It is when a European arrives and they ask 'What is your church?' where the problems begin. Many Europeans tend to respond by saying they don't have a church or they don't believe in any particular faith. More and more, volunteers are introducing themselves as atheists or agnostics. The Ghanaians always get quite a shock when they are met with such unfamiliar belief systems. So, during my time there as a Catholic, I ceased to associate my religion with all the aspects of the Irish Catholic Church. I was just like everybody else, I had a God to pray to and a place to pray to him in. I spent my Sundays in a Presbyterian Church with my new love and it never really dawned on me that this would prove a serious problem back in my Motherland. My generation was very loosely connected with the troubles of Northern Ireland. The Good Friday Agreement was the greatest landmark event associated with that and that began a long era of 'peace'. I had no reason to believe that this man was any different from me because he worshipped God in a different way and didn't pray to the Virgin Mary. However, choosing a black protestant as my boyfriend was not exactly what my parents had in mind. Apparently I had threatened my mother with this 'affliction' when I was staging my rebellious years. Here I was living out the threat. I started to think about the reaction of those at home. It hit me like all those other issues had hit me like a brick thrown into the pit of my stomach.

It seemed like an uphill battle but the time to leave Ghana was coming close and I was in no place in my life to make any decisions. So, I put all of my worries and doubts into that little box in my mind that I cherish so much I hardly open and spent my last weeks in this amazing land enjoying every moment with the children, my host family and this Ghanaian charming man who would eventually be in the past. Or not.

CHAPTER 6

―――◆◆◆―――

THE END OF THE DIRT TRACK

The sun was finally setting on my journey in Ghana and as I came to my final weeks, I started to feel the greatest sense of loss I have ever felt. In the school, the children and I had grown very close, despite the large class sizes. We had established a routine and it was working. We all looked forward to different parts of the day and they were gaining confidence for their exams. I had designed a mock exam based on their final exam with English questions testing their grammar, vocabulary and comprehension. Not all of them appreciated my efforts but I believe they benefited from it. I did warm to some students more than others and I particularly loved the characters whose cheeky wit always brought a smile to me face. The girls in the class would comment on my style every day. They would sweetly say 'wow Madame, you are so beautiful today'. It got me every time. They would ask me to sing and think I was wonderful when, in fact, I am a complete tone deaf crow (as my family and friends will support me on).

The school had been in need of renovation while I was there. The steps they climbed to get to class every day were falling apart making it very dangerous. There were no locks on the doors so they couldn't have anything decent in the building for fear of it being stolen. The place needed to be painted and restored. I had raised some funds over December, mostly from family members sending money to Ghana in place of Christmas presents. Together, we made the school look great and everyone worked so hard, the community spirit contributed as much as the paint itself. The finished product was something for us all to think about. It started me thinking at that time what a small amount of money could do in this place and that thought stayed with me until I was in a position to do something about it in Ireland.

However, before I left this beautiful land, I wanted to explore some of the other regions and to really verify if these Ghanaians were quite as wonderful as I had come to believe they were.

My first port of call (without my other half!) was the North of Ghana. This was the home of the Guan people and, they being the earliest people to come to Ghana, it was an observatory haven for me. My 'friend' came from the Akan tribe which makes up the Fante and Twi languages. The people have been very much divided and, even within their own tribe, communication is weak. A Twi speaker and a Fante speaker find it difficult to communicate and so end up with a form of 'Ghanaian Pidgin; or broken English (depending on the level of education of the people in question). As my friend on the plane told me when I fist started out on this trip, the Akan people were extremely determined and managed to comfortably live together in peace for 200 years. They then split into various groups to form their own states. There are now so many Akan sub-groups in Ghana, that the Ghanaians themselves are not sure which one they come from. In the village where I was based, the groups were defined by their Twi language and these particular groups had established themselves by the river Birim which was an important feature of the village.

This river which flowed through Oda was where I hung out on days off or weekends. To look at the river, I would never have imagined even dipping my feet in. It was a brownish, almost red colour with questionable debris floating downstream. The only traffic it saw were the hand-made wooden boats which brought bamboo and all manner of products across it to stock up the marketplaces and small children washing themselves. However, the heat of the roaring sun and the sweat pumping off my body meant I couldn't resist jumping in to cool off and to enjoy some time with the locals. Anyway, the colour was from cleaning gold pieces so it couldn't be that bad. I deserved to swim in gold after all!

The groups there were Adansi, Asante, Akwamu, Assin, Akyem, Denkyira and Twifu. The information I acquired over time was merely academic but somehow, my interest was shifting from anthropology to trying to understand certain 'culturisms' which were ingrained in my new found love. He was determined, passionate, a little bit wild and completely spiritual. It all made sense when I began to look back at the history and development of the land of Ghana. All that history in school was to teach us about the people we have become today. We treat it as so abstract but its social and cultural relevance should not be overlooked. It was the same for me here in Ghana. The more I poked for information, the greater my understanding became of behaviour that I once thought was inappropriate or impolite. Now I found most things endearing. I was still slightly annoyed with people shouting in my ear and hearing 'ssss' regularly in order to get my attention but that is something I would never get over no matter how much knowledge I had.

Passing from South to North Ghana, so many changes came to view along with the increased density of dust and smoke. The contrast was phenomenal.

As mentioned, the North was the settling ground of the earliest people in Ghana. The knowledge of these facts has only been passed on orally so it is always difficult to be completely accurate but Guan people were also supposedly settled in the areas where Fante people would settle long before the Fante people ever arrived. The Guan were said to have migrated from what is now known as Burkina Faso. Most of the Guan people are now in the Volta Regions of Ghana.

The North is predominately Muslim, stemming back to the time of cross-Sahara trade which was a catalyst for the spread of Islam to West Africa. The Muslims came from Mali and, at that time, Islam was the state religion of the Songhai Empire. (From the 15th to 16th Century, the Songhai Empire was one of the largest African empires in history). Apart from the abundance of Muslims in that region compared to the South, the wooden huts and roadside children were most noticeable. In the future I would return to this place many times and now it seems so normal but then, I felt like I had entered the Africa that everyone spoke of. The poverty was evidently prevalent and the buildings were no longer made from cement. The schools were scarce and the industries slow. The landscape is very much dictated by the weather. While in the wet season, the Northern Region experiences great flooding, the dry season leaves the land arid and dry as the Sahara itself. Northern communities (outside the cities) live in the forest but not far from the roadside. The road running through this region is relatively new and connects the South to the North over the White Volta River. These communities live in mud and straw huts in villages with populations of 10 to 100 depending on the community. As the tro tro (the white vans which are Ghana's mode of public transport) drove past, I wondered how these communities came to be. I remember reading in 'The Shadow of the Sun' by Ryszard Kapuscinski, the story of a village beginning due to a hole in the ground which so many people came to see they had to set up stalls and places to rest and eventually it became a village.

How did people decide to settle in that particular area? The schools were so far away and this made me feel hopeless as I couldn't imagine how the children would walk so far to a school and I also couldn't imagine that the teachers were as qualified as they would be in other regions.

The people here are isolated or 'non urbanised' as those in the politically correct world of anthropology call it. Their lives are as contrasting as the Ghanaian landscape. It is both intriguing and at the same time, tough. They sell pieces of fire wood on the sides of the street and as you watch the children smile as you go by, your heart melts and then freezes. It is the striking contrast of feelings and emotions that only Africa can offer.

The fire wood which they (mainly the women) sell is bought by people for the purposes of cooking and heating. Coal pots which are very common in other regions are not used here. In the dead heat of the afternoon soon, it is like a ghost town in these small villages. I didn't see anybody during the hours of 1.30 to 3.00. The wood is visible but there are no people around. Most of the men are gone to the farm in search of food. Some of the children are at school. However, most of the children are needed to work at home and so the educational process never takes off here. Sometimes, it felt like the world was moving from chapter to chapter and they are still on the first page. But then, in true African contrast, I remembered that they probably remember that first page and appreciate those words more than we do our whole book collection.

As I approached the city of Tamale, I was exposed for the first time to the prayer sessions of Muslims. One of the pillars of their faith. Five times a day they pray in the direction of Mecca and what a wonderfully disciplined act it is.

Islam, Muslim, Allah. To certain people, these words bring distain, fear and, in some cases, hatred. Tolerance is found by learning and understanding, through the ability to receive and give love, and due to lack of these basic requirements, Muslims can be misconstrued all over the world. In Ghana, where religious orders live side by side, I got the first true insight into the life of a Muslim. If they practice their faith as the Koran dictates, they are a very peaceful, disciplined, loving group of people. Not everyone lives like this in the world of Islam but then Christians do not always behave as they should.

Like the Bible, the Koran can be misinterpreted leading followers to oppress women, commit terrible atrocities and to hate all that is Christian. However, a Muslim who is true to Islam respects Christians.

Jesus Christ was a prophet in the days of Mohammed so why should he be cast aside?

Difference should not always breed contempt. I was learning this on the journey. We do not always have to accept all of the customs, especially where we feel human rights are being encroached, but understanding why they do what they do sheds a new light on them and all that can be different. Their way of worship may be different as is that of Protestant, Methodist, Jew but we are all after the same thing. Whether we believe in God or not, we are all looking for a life of peace, forgiveness and hope. That is what those who pray seek and, whether they know it or not, what those who do not pray want ultimately. The clouds come and go but we are all under the same stars.

So, the journey from Tamale wasn't Northern enough. There was even further to go. There were stories of these mysterious crocodiles in a place called Paga at the most Northern tip of Ghana almost stretching over the border for Burkina. The crocodiles are as big as you can get and I believe the species is the one that tends to eat humans when it is hungry! My less that adequate knowledge of crocodiles comes from visiting a Croc Park in Darwin, Australia and watching the late Steve Irwin. However, I do know that they are dangerous but yet these Ghanaian crocodiles were apparently as friendly as the Ghanaians themselves! People are invited to sit on them, feed them, pet them like any other domestic animal. Incredible. I wanted to see it with my own two eyes. Low and behold, there it was, people striding crocodiles. The animals were breathing but looked so placid. The crocodiles are said to be the ancestors of the Kassena tribe who inhabit the surrounding area. Each crocodile is said to represent the soul of each inhabitant. I was told a story of the hunter who came across a crocodile from Paga when he was trying to escape from the mouth of a lion. The friendly crocodile assisted him in crossing the river and ever since these animals are friendly, obliging and polite. I am sure there is another explanation that scientists insist on telling us but for the moment, it is wonderful to believe that gods and ancient ancestors can live in the souls of one of the most feared animals on earth.

So, I bonded with the gods of Paga and enjoyed every moment of it. Sitting on a crocodile is not the most relaxing activity, even if they are 'friendly'. You can't help but think that they may change their mind any moment and get a little cranky. Especially the female ones. Who doesn't know a woman who can turn at any given moment?

When all the crocodile encounters had ended, I packed up and headed down to Larabanga which leads ultimately to the very famous and beautiful Mole National Park. When the bus drops you at Larabanga, it is a mystery how to then get to the National Park.

However, like everything in Africa, it is possible. A few cedis later and a lot of negotiation, one finds oneself in a flinstonesque (a word I came up with after getting myself from one place to another by car but practically on foot!) taxi speeding over a dirt track through a sensational lush surrounding. At the top of the track stands Mole National Park visitor centre and hotel/hostel/tent.

The most striking thing about the place is its breathtaking view over the park, the rivers in the distance, the elephants plodding over the dry muck in search of water, and the most stunning of all, the African sunset in all its glory. There is a swimming pool to bathe in as you take in the view and, for a while, it feels like paradise. Then, the urge to use the bathroom comes and you find yourself back in Africa. I returned to this place a couple of times after this occasion for various reasons and I could never understand how a place that made so much money could have the most terrible facilities. It doesn't have running water so, in order to take a shower, you need to ask reception to bring buckets of water. This should cover you for showers, brushing your teeth and toilet flush. Being used to the bucket of water sanitation situation, it was not a problem for me but I was expecting more for the extortionate amount of Cedis I was paying, relatively. With regard to the water for the toilet, one just hopes that there are no extra bowel movements and that it is sufficient to last the days you intend to stay for. This is always the case for me in Ghana. Back in the village, when I needed to use the toilet, there were times when I was asked whether it was 'liquid or solid'. This determined the toilet I was brought to and if I needed to search for paper. It used to make me embarrassed but now it makes me smile. There have been occasions where I have had to ask my Ghanaian boyfriend to get me extra buckets of water to flush the toilet. This is where the level of embarrassment can heighten. You find yourself becoming very close to this person when they know your exact toilet habits.

Mole lacked all the essential basic facilities but what it lacked in that area it made up for I its sheer location and accessibility to Africa's greatest animals.

A morning safari walk, which costs less than 60cent, is a fantastic way to take in the surrounding area. A guide walks you through the African plains describing the animals spotted on the way and tracking elephants. The greatest imaginable image is that of a herd of elephants right in front of you in their own inhabitant getting on with their daily business. The mixture of fear, adrenalin and amazement takes over and it is a moment never to be forgotten. I wasn't sure what to do with all the emotions running through me. I suddenly wanted to share this moment and so I found myself making a phone call to the one person I wanted to share it with. I spoke to him about what I had done and seen and how much I missed him and wanted him to be here. Like all natives, we never really visit our own country to the full like we do when we visit others. He was the same. He had heard of all these places but had never gone to that part of Ghana for anything other than business and certainly not as a tourist.

After Mole, I headed back down to the kingdom of Kumasi in central Ghana. This is the place which holds an abundance of history stemming all the way back to 1640. It is still a monarchy today and represents the highest level of chieftain hierarchy.

Having traced world speech patterns and word usage, ethno linguists have confirmed that the Ashanti migrated form the Niger River area around the 13th Century. The Ashanti are known for their display of great riches having come from their trade of gold with other major empires.

During the 17th Century, the Ashanti used their military power to unite all the clans under one chief (Chief Oti Akenten) without taking away the power of the clan chiefs themselves. Prior to this unity of Ashanti clans, the region had been under the control of the Denkyira.

The most important symbol of the Ashanti is the Golden Stool. According to legend, this stool was commanded down from the heavens by Okomfop Anokye under the rule of the first king (Asantehene Osei Tutu I). The Golden Stool then floated down from the heavens into the lap of the king. It was then declared the symbol of the new Asante Union. With the strength of this union bound by the stool, the Ashanti went to war against the Denkyira and achieved their independence. The Stool now reigns as an extremely precious, sacred item as it is said to contain the 'Sunsum' which is the spirit or soul of the Ashanti people.

No other people in Ghana benefited from the wealth that their resources, including humans, created. The Ashanti kingdom hold great importance in Ghana. They benefited from all that was tragic about the country's past. The area was rich in gold, ivory and the trading of slaves. It is mainly through the profits of this slave trade that allowed the Ashanti to become a dominating force in West Africa.

We are always quick to criticise colonisation, and it is of course an imperialistic ideal which has destroyed many lives, on the basis that it disturbed what was once a peaceful nation going about their own business. However, the division of wealth, greed, exploitation of resources and land occupation was taking place within nations prior to colonial expeditions. The Ashanti fought off every African group who tried to gain access to their wealth. This followed with years of Ashanti wars. They fought the Fante people, then the Ga people, then the Akim-Akwapim alliance who occupied the coastal regions.

Inevitably, this level of wealth became increasingly tempting to British traders who saw this as an opportunity to access the wealth of West Africa. However, it took four wars to defeat the Ashanti. They resisted the British until in 1896, when Britain annexed the Ashanti territories and they were sent into exile in the Seychelles. The coastal regions were then declared the Gold Coast colony, a British resident was set up permanently and soon a fort would be built to really put the word out that the land belonged to the British Empire. It would never be apparent in Kumasi that the British had taken over for so many years. It looks like an ancient kingdom around where the palace is; gold items all around reminding us that there was once a very powerful kingdom present.

However the powerful this kingdom may have been, I don't believe it was all that much compared to the market that surrounds Kumasi. It is the largest market I have ever seen in all my travelling years and all my time in African markets. The smells that come from it are so difficult to take that there are moments when I felt I would collapse. There is nothing that you can not get in that market. On a Saturday when I needed to change Euro and the banks were closed, a very nice man offered to make me a 'sweet deal' and actually changed my money at a good rate. Having lived in Ireland, where the post office closes for lunch and the bank only has one teller on at the busiest time over that period, dealing with African markets is a breath of fresh air—well maybe not *fresh* air, but efficient air.

The next time I would be in Kumasi, it would save a friend's life.

After Kumasi, I made my way to the Volta region. The Volta region, which is accessible from Akosombo ferry port, is a really beautiful place.

Lake Volta is the largest man-made lake in the world. As the ferry leaves the port, the lake looks like something from a different world, mystical. A lake but yet not real and covered by mist which I had never seen in Ghana before. It is so calm and clear but the water doesn't make any sound as the boat penetrates through it. I was fascinated by this magical journey. It was honestly like a scene from the *Chronicles of Narnia*.

However, upon arrival at Volta, the hotel there is prepared for people who think this is 'amazing' and are willing to pay for the pleasure. I wasn't exactly rolling in cash at the time and I was living by Ghanaian economics so I was not overly impressed by the top class service on offer! After a few cocktails (at full Western prices) and some nice Italian meals (which were not as nice as Ghanaian dishes—but don't tell the Italians), I left the Volta region and headed back in the direction of Cape Coast.

Cape Coast is a region that I paid a lot of attention to. It is the home of the slave trade where castles were built by Portuguese, Dutch and British colonial powers to hold and subsequently export slaves to Latin America, Europe and other parts of the world.

On my third visit to Ghana, I learned much more about this region and I was much more comfortable. The first time I visited it, I was conscious of my skin colour as it is the one area in Ghana where people remember the plight the white man caused them. There is an air of bitterness about the place and the Ghanaian friendliness so prevalent in other parts of the country is lacking around the castles of Elmina and Cape Coast. The colonial scars are ever prevalent around this area especially. I asked some people in my circle of friends what they felt about colonialism. My 'boyfriend' explained it to me as everything is explained—through the medium of parable, proverb of ancient story. It is a beautiful way to learn and it always made my research so delightful. So, he lets me know that if you give a man a gun and he shoots his father we may of course blame the man, but the one who has given him the gun is equally responsible. So, in reference to the imperial nature of Western colonialism, it appears that the Africans gave the settlers what they wanted to destroy them. He believes Africans were tempted by what the Westerners had to offer and were, in turn, the propagators of the game of chess subsequently played by European leaders. When the first explorers came to Africa, they saw that in the rituals of the ancient African tribes, libation was used in ceremonies. It was a form of Schnapps. So, when the Europeans realised how precious this form of 'alcohol' was to the natives, the bartering could begin. The African, albeit unaware of the value of the products it was sitting on, happily gave over the diamond and gold in exchange for alcohol. Over time, African tribes oppressed other African tribes and the destruction of the land, pillaging of the people, separation of clans, was not only down to the West, but also the natives themselves must take some responsibility. Colonialism would probably have happened anyway but it would not have been called that—it would have been called civil war.

After Cape Coast, it was time to return to the village and say my final goodbyes to all of those people who had been dear to my heart during my time in this country.

I was more looking forward to this trip than any I had had in the previous 2 weeks and it wasn't to say goodbye. It was to see a face I knew I wouldn't forget very easily.

When I arrived back to the village, I immediately went to the market stall where I would see him again. There he stood genuinely delighted that I was back and I beamed up at him form the lower step I was on and forgot everything that was going on around us.

We arranged to meet that evening as I was due to travel to Accra in 2 days time to fly back home.

That evening, I met with all the friends I had made and we celebrated my journey and life until the early hours of the morning. We all knew, when the volunteers left, they very rarely returned and we toasted to the holiday romance I had had with their good friend, to the children I had taught, to the lives I had affected and to my life being affected.

They made me promise not to forget them in Ireland and to always hold them in their hearts.

The next day I travelled to Accra with my ever loving companion by my side. We were due to stay in a hotel as my flight was the next day and I had wanted to be sure I would be there so staying in Accra was the easiest way to do that.

It would be the first time alone together in a room—a bedroom at that. The nerves ran through me like a first day at school, or a job interview. When I saw the double bed in the room, I didn't know how to react. There were expectations there that had not been there before. I was, at first, angry at the assumption, but when that dissipated, I felt excited, alive, it felt comfortable. Suddenly, sharing a room with this man seemed like the right thing to do. I let go of the feelings of anxiety and uncertainty that had empowered my body and mind and laid my self bare in every sense of the expression.

It was my last night in Ghana and it was wonderful. I kept a sense of detachment inside of me always aware of the looming trip home and the final goodbye.

When it was time to leave the following day, I was actually quite positive. We spoke about how wonderful our time together was and how we would leave our fate in the hands of God. If we were meant to be together, we would find the strength inside ourselves to allow that to happen. We would use the tools at our disposal to make it possible. For now, it was a distant idea; one that we both knew would be extremely difficult and highly unlikely.

The final kiss goodbye melted me more than the heat of the Ghanaian afternoon sun. I disappeared into a dream and when he left me at Kotoka Airport, Accra, I felt my heart sink so far into my body that I almost fainted. I walked into the departure lounge all set for the long journey home.

The first tears came when the Lufthansa flight attendant showed me to my seat. The tears dried up when I touched down in Dublin.

Chapter 7

Where the heart is

I was home. Most anthropologists study cultural assimilation (blending into another culture when you are not a native) and integration from the point of view of a foreigner in a new setting. The other, less explored theory, looks at how the native blends back into their own environment when they return home, a form of reverse culture shock.

I had expected Ghanaian life to be so different, and it was. I knew the food would taste strange to me, and it did. I new the people would behave unusually compared to the Irish and I knew the culture would shock me to the core. It all happened as I expected but I learned to deal with it, to adapt, to embrace the magic of change and it worked. I had learned so many things about African life and I loved it. I had experienced the hardship and the difficulty in the education system, the poverty and the every day struggle to survive. I had witnessed it, not lived it, but it stayed with me. It always does.

However, back in Ireland, I hadn't prepared for the difficulty in re-adapting, even after the short amount of time I had been away. I am not a person who has ever suffered from depression. I always find a way to shake it off. That Christmas I came home, I felt an emptiness in myself that I had never experienced before. Ireland seemed different to me somehow. I started to sense all the typical clichés and stereotypes people mention after living in a Third World country. I saw the lack of appreciation we had for everything we touched. The quest for survival starts from a very early age in Ghana. For us, survival is about fastening our seatbelts or avoiding walking in the dark at night for fear of a rapist or murderer who will steal our life. It is about preserving a life of privilege for some and existential being. The children in Ghana put themselves in harms way for a quest which doesn't preserve a life but allows a life to go on. For many, going to school means having a job that may allow your family to have three meals a day. Selling anything and everything means putting food on the table and prolonging life for a time in the foreseeable future. When the children carry the water or other items for hours in the dead heat, it is not questioned. It is an instinct which takes over their minds and with a few beads of sweat and a smile they get on with it.

The humility which is brought with such actions is overwhelming. I can not really compare life in the West to how they life their lives. We have different ways of appreciating life, of course, and a different sense of values and beliefs. But, at the time I arrived back from Ghana, these thoughts took over my conscious and subconscious.

Life is tough there I thought. The children dream of becoming footballers and providing for their families and villages. I felt a sense of inherent jealousy of the pureness they live in. They have no time for building barriers of values. The search for the basics has brought joy in every simple thing. When we release all the tensions of modern life here, are we not like these children, enlightened by all that is great around us. Don't get me wrong, progression is what we strived for and, in many ways some of our lives are easier due to our advances in technology, economics and resource management. However, looking around what felt like a foreign land, I could not help but think that maybe the price of modernisation is too much. Maybe, if they paid the price for progression, they would lose their Africanism that is so special to them. Maybe, I had lost some of my 'Irishness' that was so special to me. Perhaps, children here have too much so that it takes more to bring a light to their smile. And, sometimes, here you see people who grow up sleeping (in De Mello terms), walking into financial doors, property ladders or falling into traps of the latest invention or gadget. Most of us do not want to be like the Africans, the very people we donate money to when we can because we feel pity, but, maybe, we should slow down and try to learn from them in other ways. They allow us to share our wealth with them, but they should share their appreciation of life with us, their spirituality. In the words of Anthony De Mello 'The nature of the rain is the same but thorns grow in the marshes and flowers in the garden'.

I was consumed by these ideas and I wanted to let them all go and get on with whatever normality I had before this adventure. I wanted to enjoy Irish life which I always had before instead of comparing it to my experiences and complaining about it.

Christmas was tough but I enjoyed the time with my family. I missed the people I had left in Ghana and the children at the school. On Christmas day, I made a call to my host mother in the village and wished everyone a Happy Christmas (even though as Jehovah Witnesses, they dispelled the date of Christmas as hearsay). It was wonderful to hear them. Then I placed a call to a man I missed the most. Hearing his voice made me feel whole again for the first time in weeks. We spoke for 30 minutes and at the end of it, I knew it was going to take hard work, a lot of will power and a lot of dates with other suitors to get him out of my head.

And so time passed and I went further and further into myself. I was out partying to cover the feelings gnawing away at me. I was defeating the whole purpose of having gone away and going back to my old ways. I thought I had learned so much more but it was taking time to all sink in. I started dating people again. I was still in contact with Ghana and when things were not going my way, I would call my 'Ghanaian friend' for advice and he would tell me to keep strong and that he loved me. I knew I had to make a hard decision. I told him we needed to cut contact and that was to be my final encounter with him.

I thought it had worked. I went about my daily routine, eating like there was no tomorrow, piling on weight, oversleeping, drinking, anything that distracted me.

Eventually it all got too much and I called him again and told him I missed speaking with him and maybe I was a bit hasty in my plea for him to never call me again.

And so, we began a long distance friendship that turned into something extremely refreshing and natural.

Shortly after arriving in Ireland, I began to think about what could be done for the schools in the area where I had worked. They had asked me to do what I could when I returned and I had made a promise. So I began to think of starting an NGO (Non-Governmental organisation). With the help of a friend and the support of people around, we applied to the government for recognition and tax exemption. It wasn't the easiest thing in the world. In fact, the paperwork involved would become quite a nightmare. You just keep saying that the end justifies the means. It was necessary to put together objectives, projections and a business plan structure. It was great for us also to see exactly what realistic goals could be met in the time we had outlined. The proposal went back and forth for months but eventually we were certified as Dinka Ireland. We chose the name Dinka simply because we knew it to be an African tribe from Sudan and we liked the sound of it. It was a proud moment and the launch came before the economy of Ireland crashed and burned so we started out well.

Our first mission was to build a school in the village where I had worked. We knew there were a few sites ready for the construction of a school and that there were hundreds of children waiting to get premises to build a future for themselves that only education can afford.

A year had passed by the time the NGO was set up, money was raised and plans were put in place. It had been a strange year and in some ways, the NGO had been a distraction which allowed me to think of Ghana and distract me from my heart which was growing fonder. The long distance relationship which was now truly something incredible was preventing me from enjoying dates or giving my heart away. I was in constant conflict of emotion and denial but I was determined not to allow my heart to guide me into a life full of uncertainty and difficulty. I had to continuously reassure my parents that this man was a voice (of reason) on the phone and that it would never become reality. I repeated it so often, I made myself believe it.

As we raised the money, we now needed to research exactly where the new primary school was going to go.

So the time had arrived to return to Ghana after 14 months of living in some sort of twilight. I, again, had to question all of my motives. I definitely knew that the school was a mission I was going to take seriously, laced with echoes of romantic notions which I knew were also motivating my next trip to the West African nation I loved so much.

When the flight was booked, veins had been poisoned with diseases apparently prevalent in Ghana (money scam if ever I saw one) and all the finances for the NGO were in place, it was time to prepare myself.

Could I better prepare myself this time round? Preparation is futile really. We can not really prepare ourselves for these things. We just have to be open to anything, and take it as it comes. I was learning as I went along. I would just accept what was about to come and pray that I would be strong enough to recognise any signs that were to come my way. This is the hard part of life. Whether or not we believe in God, there are still signs around us and, if we fail to see them for what they are, certain things may pass us by. If we are open to external indicators in our path through life, we may see them and make the decisions that allow us to live life to the full. So, this was the kind of thoughts I took with me on this journey. I just wanted to remain open. I was going to begin a school building project and it had to be about the community where the school was being built. There would be no place for egos taking over. The power a person can achieve from being in a position to provide a school for other people could be phenomenal. I had to keep focus on the reason for doing this. We had raised some money. The village needed a school. The community would take on the project and we would provide some cash. That was it. That was all it was.

I still have a power struggle with the concept. I am still very much involved with raising money for schools in West Africa but since Ireland's economical collapse, I watched people around me suffer 'Western poverty'. A new form of poverty hit me and most of those in my native country. Suddenly, after growing up in Bertie's Celtic Tiger (the prime minister which we call 'Taioseach' of the time who spent money loosely during Ireland's economic boom), I found myself, friends and family wondering if they could pay their bills. I had friends who were once architects and were now applying to St. Vincent De Paul for toys for their family.

It was a new world. It was worse than African poverty because they had never known what it was like to have it. We had it and lost it. We lived on credit and got whatever it was whenever we wanted it. But it was all changing around the time I was going to Ghana. I had to question whether we white people were actually in a position to help people who were now bemused by Europe's inability to plan or control its finances. Africans I spoke to asked me how banks and governments were unable to forward plan or make provision for rainy days. The word 'poverty' that had always echoed through the acacia trees of the African plains was now running off the tongues of white people.

The Catholic Church was fighting for its own redemption after plagues of abuse allegations so they were unavailable for counselling.

I wondered before that journey if we were fooling ourselves to think we could assist anybody. We had made a mess of it. There was no doubting it, however, whatever state we were in, we had the basic infrastructure in place and basic human rights were being made. I was always proud of the education system in Ireland, and it was one area which I was familiar and I knew it worked. Our schools had been doing something right and, having seen the hunger for learning in the eyes of Ghanaian children, I knew providing education may be the key to a bright future for them. Maybe, in the future, the Ghanaians may have an opportunity to come to Europe and teach us something!

It was with that final thought that I would keep with me if I was to take on this challenge.

Taking an hour off work, I went to get my Ghanaian visa and my shots.

I took off for Accra, this time with my Dinka partner for the second time. Would he be there when I got off that plane and how would I feel if he was?

CHAPTER 8

—◆→◉←◆—

OBSERVATIONS

It doesn't get easier, it just gets more familiar. The words of a singer I once heard from Belgium. It said it all on my second trip back to the land of Akwaba and fufu. I had landed and, even though I experienced the same obstacles as the first time, including being ripped off by a taxi driver and melting in the heat of the African sun, I was somehow more tolerant and accepting. Experience speaks wonders in any context. The first picture which always incites my thoughts and emotions is that of the Ghanaian children. It is always a huge disparity of African versus the West. One of the most intriguing and challenging sights in Africa is the treatment of children. In the Western world, where abuse or neglect are not considered, we generally protect our children and worship them in a way. We just have to observe how a conversation unfolds between a teenager and her or his mother on a phonecall during rush hour rail service. It may go : 'shut up Mom, I told you already I was staying in my friend's house' . . . 'well Mom, I can do what I like now, I am 13'.

I have heard it with my own ears and didn't pay all that much attention to it until I hit the ground covered in African soil. From day one, our babies are wrapped in blankets—the ultimate metaphorical symbol of pure protection. (Some finding it hard to peel off as the years go by). For many, they are handled with extreme caution, toddlers watched at every moment, in every movement. The proverbial 'you can't take your eyes off them for a moment' ringing in every mother's ear. The plugs in the house are covered, sharp objects removed. Some parents follow their toddlers around while their nerves dangle on a thin wire.

71

It goes without saying that the majority of Western children are sent to school as soon as legally possible. Often, they are picked up, dropped off and God forbid if anyone touches them!

Imagine now, in the Ghanaian way (and probably, most of Africa from my experience) the complete opposite. The love the people have for their children here is not in question. Ghanaian children are loved but they are treated in a very different way. Babies seem to be hardy from a very early age and they are taught to fend for themselves. It is the very traditional method of survival, in some ways, animalistic. The child must learn to survive in order to succeed in the difficult journey that is life. This time in Ghana, I was handed a baby on the way through customs in Accra before leaving the airport. A baby was handed to me and I had no idea who its parents may be. She was adorable and I held her, examining her wire—like curls and deep eyes. She was then passed around a few more times until the mother eventually returned from the toilet. She had not worried about her child being stolen or dropped. Pure trust and no blanket in sight!

From the cradle to the grave, it is felt that God is the greatest protector so whatever will happen will happen. Girls from the age of 5 or 6 learn to survive very quickly. They are responsible for fetching the water and other items, washing up, cleaning and lighting fires. As they grow, so too do their duties. Girls of 9 to 13 are on the streets selling whatever they can carry in their heads—water, rice, fish, toothpaste or even cement! Many of them do not attend school. The girls can really wash clothes. It always fascinated me to watch them clean better that my machine while my knuckle bled from one piece of underwear! It was one thing I would never adapt to in all my African lifespan. The children fan the fires for hours in order for their mothers' to cook. They use sharp knives to cut the food, cutlasses to mow the lawn and they walk everywhere alone—even in the darkest hours of the night. Boys are less concerned with what are known as 'menial tasks' and their association with food comes only in the form of pounding fufu. Muscles are needed for this task and, this, in case you were wondering, is how the men in Ghana always look they spend hours in a gym when in fact most have never seen the inside of one! Boys build bridges, new houses, roads. They mend cars with the most dangerous of tools.

School is no haven for these children of Ghana. Their typical school day involves working physically and mentally. Teachers seem to look for reasons to punish them without the worry of an angry parent waiting to pounce. Teachers are constantly prodding them, provoking responses which merit the lash of a cane at times (although this is legally not permitted anymore in Ghana). They are spoken down to and required to show respect at all times. The respect in Ghana between a young person or child and an adult is never broken. It is simply unheard of.

The two ends of the spectrum couldn't be further apart. The difference is overwhelming and something I find difficult in both worlds. I find African children are sometimes treated as slaves but I also find Western children treated as Kings. Again I am back to this questioning of happy mediums.

While Africa moves towards growth and development, there is not much that can be done to assist the children as the way they do things here is what they see as right and we are in no position to question that.

For the moment, in Ghana, the relief comes from knowing that whatever the children are doing here, they are always doing it with a smile.

As my thoughts about the Ghanaian way of life subsided, I focused on what awaited me outside and suddenly I couldn't feel myself breathing anymore.

CHAPTER 9

A ROSE IS A ROSE BY ANY OTHER NAME

His name is Kwabena. It flows off my tongue like water from the mountain. He was given this name on account of the day in which he arrived on this earth. As a male, if it had been a Monday, he would have been Kwadwo but then again on a Wednesday, the visitors would have been admiring Kwaku. The Thursday born is left with quite an usual phonetic and it tends to be more of a stutter than an African name. Thursday children are automatically Yaw. My own day, which I happen to share with the former UN secretary of State, Mr. Kofi Annan is Friday. Kofi is a very popular Ghanaian name (the female version and my permanent name in Ghana is Afia). Saturday males are very important as it is said that God himself was born on a Saturday. The great freedom fighter and leader of independent Ghana is Kwame Nkrumah so Kwame rings through as a powerful name and I have come across many of them during my time in this country. Sunday is Kwasi and also significant in his shared interest with the holy day. These people are said to be more relaxed due to their birth name.

Of the 7 days in the week, I now had found new value in Tuesday. Of course, the Ghanaians are given other names although, it is still possible to listen to people discuss ten different Kwames in a conversation and one has to decipher the dialogue.

The other names given are usually Biblical in Christian circles or Koranic in Muslim circles. As it is unlikely to come across any atheists in this part of the Southern Hemisphere, there are no Britney's, Brad's or Paddy's. Then the names come from a Grandmother (usually matriarchal in Africa). So a person may be called Kwame Emmanuel Opoku Asomoah.

So, there he stood looking radiant in the light of the African sunset. His top buttons undone, where a dark smooth chest emerged and the tiny beads of sweat sparkled and faded like diamonds in the river. All the time, I walked that distance from the plane to the arrival gate I told myself to be open, that it was time to face reality and that I was here to shed light on a situation that was fictional, unattainable and outright madness!

When his eyes met mine I knew there was love but the pragmatism of an Irish woman on the 'right' side of societal victimisation was shining through. I would be strong and not succumb to the charms of this Ghanaian Adonis. I would not submit as an African woman, there was a strength I had that came with experience of rejecting and being rejected. So, I walked on free to choose. That is what I realised when I looked back at this time. I didn't really understand that that was what I had to do. We are really here to choose all the time. Everything is a choice. Someone may say, 'but what about a mother who has a small child to look after, what choice does she have? It is not only herself to think of'. However harsh as it may seem she could leave the baby somewhere and move away if she chose to do that. It may not be a choice any of us would consider but the point is that it is choice. If you choose to keep that baby, as hard as that may be, you must live with that choice.

We drove back to the hotel where we were staying and a deep sense of awkwardness took over. Nobody really knew what was going to happen. Whatever would take place, we were here to distribute funds for the building of a school and that would take priority.

As we awakened to the usual sounds of a familiar nature, it was time to travel to the village.

CHAPTER 10

CHIEFS

We were due to visit some sites which had been acquired by different villages through the influence of the chiefs. The land would be left barren after that if there were no funds to begin a project. The loyalty and enthusiasm of a chief was something which perplexed me to some degree during the initial investigation into a school to fund. I believed that perhaps the chiefs were using their power for their self importance, the benefits of diplomatic visas which allowed them to travel around the world or for status. Kwabena convinced me that the chiefs may live in bigger houses than their villagers, they may have more money and higher standards of living but that they do use their influences wisely. If they were to give their money away to build houses and schools and then when they themselves become poor, what would the sense be? Everyone should suffer and no good to come out? So I stood corrected and turned my attention to the behaviour required when one meets an African chief and I carried myself as best I could but unknowing how my behaviour was going to go down,

The Chiefs are not elected by general vote, nor are they part of the government. In fact, the Ghanaian Constitution prohibits chiefs from becoming politicians.

In order to attain the high honour, a person is required to have royal blood running through their veins. Your name must echo the title of royal families past or present. It does not matter which country or how your family may have behaved but that you have a name connected to a royal family. (Of course, money always helps in these situations and chiefs have been known to flatter the village elders with the colour green and a distant name of royal descent).

As soon as you have put yourself forward and your name has been confirmed as royal, the elders of the village set about electing you to become chief.

It is an important selection. These chiefs or kings (as many Ghanaians call them) are the rulers of the land. Before the white man came, they were the people in charge, to be more respected than anyone in the country.

Although chiefs can not be in government, there is a connection with the ruling party. Some chiefs are given diplomatic status which allows them to travel in the interest of their community. When decisions have to be made on village business, the chief must bring a proposal to the district assembly which then gets sent on to a member of parliament where a decision is likely to be made.

From all the different villages I have visited in Ghana over the years, it is amazing how different practices are in place depending, quite often, on the nature of the chief and very independent from the governing of the land. In the West, usually, society is structured on the rules applied by Government decisions and the Constitution. We know what is right and what is wrong (whether all of us practice that or not). In Ireland, people in the capital Dublin are under the same societal limitations as those in the counties of Cork or Galway. We use know what behaviour is acceptable and we are conscious of this requirement.

However, being ruled by chiefs in African villages, there are times you think you stepped into an ancient world having just come from the urban jungle. In Eastern Ghana particularly, there are some rituals and customs practiced by the villagers that make the culture intriguing and often difficult to fathom. For example, in the Eastern region, there is a practice called 'Bragoro'. It is a ceremony practiced among Akan tribes in this part of the country. It involves a young girl's initiation into womanhood taking place just after the girl's first menstruation. While the girls may be quite young, the practice is justified by the emphasis on keeping them pure and safe. Girls from the age of 13 onwards are brought from the innocence of their virgin years and offered to a potential husband. The ceremony itself is fascinating. The ceremony coincides with cocoa season, a significant time in the life of a Ghanaian. The Queen mother of the village (a female chief in this case given the nature of the ritual) examines the girl to make sure that the requirements for the initiation are met. The girl is then placed on a stool with a white cloth on her head. Relatives and friends make a semi-circle around her singing, clapping and dancing in the way Africans only know how. Food and other items are supplied by these relatives usually in the form of palm oil, money, yams or eggs.

The girl is them smeared with shea butter which is a beautiful cream made of natural ingredients similar to coco butter. She is then carried on someone's back and taken to be bathed in the river. She is given yams and eggs. 12 eggs are cooked but the girl is forbidden from chewing the eggs as this is seen as 'chewing away her fertility' and completely against the rules. The only alternative then remains—to swallow them!

The ceremony continues as the girl is blind-folded and asked to touch one of the children present at the process. The sex of this chosen child will determine the sex of her first born. In Africa, everything can be pre-determined and always induces such hope in the hearts of the people. If we never allow anything to be determined, then we never really see it happening and can never celebrate it until the time comes. These people celebrate what is and what is to come.

Following from choosing the sex of the child, a party ensues and continues for hours. At the end of the party, the girl is taken to a 'Brafie' or a large hut for 7 days to be shown the responsibilities of womanhood. This is usually facilitated by a female elder.

In this ceremony, let it be known that no genital mutilation or circumcision take place. It is devoid of any pain. 2 years ago in Ghana a law was passed banning genital mutilation. It does, however, take place in some tribes but I have not come across any cases in my time in Ghana. Knowing about this type of ritual and others gave me an idea of the role that the chiefs played and the kind of culture I was dealing with. This was my way of arming myself while going about the 'business' I had come here to do. It helped me to remember how traditional things can be in this part of Ghana and I had to respect that.

In order to decide on a site to commence the school building, we visited 3 sites. This meant speaking to 3 chiefs.

Knowing the mixed reviews I had heard about Chiefs running their villages I entered into negotiations with slight trepidation and overwhelming naiveté. The first village (all centred around the same area where I had previously promised to assist in whatever way I could) was an interesting prospector. The school seemed to be very well equipped but was in need of extra classrooms and restoration on the roof. This was the place where I always remember my anal retention was put to the test and I was forced to divulge the greatest secret kept between a woman and the inner workings of the body. I remember arriving at the school and desperately needed to what the Ghanaians constantly refer to as 'urinate'. My stomach was acting up too and in Africa one can never be too sure as to what may happen on a trip to the 'toilet'. I informed the headmaster of my desire and was questioned over the nature of the impending visit. The conversation went something like this.

'Excuse me, could you please show me where the toilet is please?'

'Yes, Madame, of course. Are you passing fluid or solid?'

'Just fluid, thanks'

I think this would have been my response no matter what but now I would be brought to the appropriate toilet based on my response.

As I continued to assess the needs of this school, I and the Ghanaian Pastor who accompanied me thought that it was doing fine on its own.

This particular structure represented the potential the new Ghana had. Under the previous President, John Kufour, the country had thrived in many ways despite the usual political fallbacks of most governments, namely corruption, neglect to certain areas etc. The new President at that time, John Mills was just coming to power during my first few times in the country so I am yet to see how the country continues to progress under his government. (Since finishing this book, John Mills did not finish his first term as he died from throat cancer and was succeeded by John Dramani Mahama). I would love to see him spread the education fund to the rural parts of the country so that the overexpansion of the capital Accra could slow down and people may actually want to stay in their home villages and be proud to send their child to one of its schools.

For the moment, this school had been given sufficient uniforms, books and the facilities were relatively modern. The unfinished building which they insisted they needed urgently did not seem to be affecting the learning potential of the children.

So, it was decided that this project was not urgent for the little money that we could supply.

The next place we visited was a school site and from the very first moment we saw it and the potential in it, we knew it was a worthy project. The site had been purchased by the people of the community. The children who would benefit from the site were 180 JSS (Junior Secondary School) students. They were currently studying in a rented building in the village that did not have enough space to hold them. There were 4 to 5 children at 1 table sharing 1 book. Some were outside as there was no room for them inside. There was no store room so the excess books and limited materials were spread across numerous classrooms, floors and spilling finally in the headmaster's room which looked like an attic full of unwanted rubbish that nobody has the heart or time to throw out at home.

The plan for the site looked ambitious and I allowed my inexperience and excitement to sign up to something that I didn't even know whether I could achieve or not.

The ego played a huge part in all of this and only on reflection was this obvious to me. These moments of invincibility prevented humility form showing its face and before I knew it, I was giving out promises like they were free samples and allowing myself to get swallowed in the moment. In my defence, I did only want to make this project work for all the right reasons. However, clouded judgement prevented me from analysing the enormous scale of building a school from scratch with no background knowledge in construction.

One thing I do know about myself, I am not afraid to say I am unfamiliar or lacking in knowledge in certain areas. I had to admit to myself that my part would be the fundraising and development of the NGO. All building design, material acquirement, staff hiring and everything else would have to be entrusted to people who did know about them.

It became a wonderful time of community involvement. Only when I had let go of the control of the project and allowed it to take course did the enjoyment come. Like anything in this world, we always feel like we want to control what goes on inside and outside of us. We soon learn that we cannot control everything but we can control how we feel about it. This revelation would come to bite me on many occasions after this moment. Whatever happened with this project, it was out of my control. It couldn't become something of an obsession. Things could go wrong, people can let you down, money does not always come easily. So, while I had to do everything in my power to make it work, becoming a charity 'diva' was not high on my list.

The first thing to do in this situation was look at the plans for the school with the local carpenter and mason to see if it could be achieved and how much it would cost. Kwabena was our interpreter to begin with but would play a massive role in the project as time went on.

The initial estimate was huge, looking at somewhere between €12000 and €15000 which was unimaginable to me. After a very heated discussion, as would only be seen in African culture, it was decided that we would acquire a permit and use the wood from the local forest to build the structure and furniture. This was to save thousands. We had previously been given another quote from other carpenters which was more and when they saw how much we were actually willing to pay, they came back with a much lower price. We had already committed to the second group at this point. The cost was now looking at around €8000 which could be done. This was back at the time when the world economy was crashing and we had no idea how this would affect the African market. The idea that inflation would rise so significantly did not enter my analysis at that time.

I began to learn how to build a structure and I became part of the day to day project. It was one of the most significant times in my life. We worked with the community and through unity and hard work it only took hours before the potential of this school could be seen.

I had gone out to Ghana having raised €3000 to start something. I was then due to go home and collect the rest. The money had been raised by holding an 'International Food Night' and I had asked all my international students at the school I worked in to bring dishes from their countries. I asked my family to prepare Irish food which my mother did a great job of. I prepared Ghanaian food and I invited all my African contacts to do dishes from their continent. The raffle was also a great money maker and I had friends donate wonderful prizes. My father had been a lighthouse keeper and I used those contacts to acquire a helicopter trip as the top prize! It went down a treat.

With the initial funding, Kwabena got great deals on cement and we began making trips back and forth with a driver to deliver the cement to the site. Trips of sand were also needed which apparently is essential in building such a structure. The cement was dropped off at the site to the labourers hired from the surrounding village. The women and children brought the water to mix the cement and in 2 afternoons, hundreds of bricks had been built. The resourcefulness of these people fascinated me. Everything was made from scratch and such strength and resilience.

I had been wondering about how to get water to the site more accessibly and, to my astonishment, my question was answered the following day. 2 very strong men took it upon themselves to dig a hole. Not just any hole. The hole went on for meters; in fact it went on until they found water. It may not have been long more before striking oil the way they were going! When water emerged, they put clean stones over the water which would act as a filter and the water could then be used in the school and eventually brought through to use when the toilets were constructed toilets. It was genius.

The women were also responsible for bringing food to the men as the site was quite far from the centre of the village.

One day, I arrived at the site quite late in the evening and found that the men had not had anything to eat from the morning to that moment. It sparked something in me.

Kwabena would see a side to me he never thought possible. While I was working through my journey of letting go of that which I could not control, there were 'slight' tantrums. If I were to be a patient of Freud, it would appear that being the youngest of 7 children with a huge age gap allows for potentially spoiled brat behavior which can show its ugly face now and again.

This is an example of how we allow ourselves to be consumed by events around us. I got angry and went on quite a rant at the Pastor in charge. Normally, the Pastor was so good at running what was happening on the site and I had a wonderful relationship with him. However, on this occasion, he had not seen to it that the women would bring up food and allowed the men to work all day in that heat without food. I just felt so bad for them and I took it out on the wrong person. It was not necessarily his fault as the men could have requested food. Hindsight is such a great thing! Kwabena told me to calm down which made me twice as bad. From that moment, he always told me he would tell me to get more riled up rather than calm down after my reaction. This didn't help the mood either. I sometimes found the heat overbearing and added with hunger and hormones, it was not a pretty sight.

Anyway, the situation was resolved, I apologized for my reaction and it never happened again. The work went on.

CHAPTER 11

DECISIONS

There is no perfect place to really think and to truly come to the decisions that affect our lives. Some choose to go to a church, bow their head and try to find the answers. Some choose meditation, in a quiet room, full of candles, scents and soothing chants. It may be the walls of your room or even the place by the sea that you went to as a child.

Somehow, the African road was my place of solitude. The tro-tro, although full of unsettled animals and the sounds of parts coming undone allowed me to look out onto the plains on the dirt track stretching towards the blurry horizon.

People do not speak on a journey in Ghana. The first thing that happens when you enter the van is a prayer. A preacher will enter before the journey to pray for the safe arrival of everyone inside. When I first experienced this, I was terrified. This man begins to shout and scream and nobody bats an eyelash. I sat in my seat the first time looking around to see if there was a reaction from anyone. All heads were bowed in prayer and I understood what was happening. I thought that maybe I should not take it for granted that without the help of God, I would arrive safely at my destination. I suddenly realised that I needed to be grateful for everything and never assume that I would wake up on the morning and go to bed that same night. This was the mentality I was coming to learn so much about and to embrace in a way I never I thought I would. It was quite powerful.

So, here I was, on yet another tro-tro journey to a village called Nkwantanang. Like any other journey, I prayed with my fellow Ghanaians and left my life in the hands of the man above.

As soon as the journey began, I looked out the window as we passed from village to village and my mind drifted as always into the abyss of subconscious thought and, before the van arrived in the village, I had made a major decision.

Throughout the process of choosing a school to build, visiting the different chiefs and proceeding with the project, I had spent quality time with Kwabena. He had told me I was the woman for him and how much he loved me. I chose at the time not to deal with it as I was due to go home in a few weeks. Here, on this trip, I found myself wondering, for the first time, what life would be like with this Ghanaian man. I asked myself why I had really come back to Ghana. I knew the school project was important to me but somewhere deep inside, I also knew my reason for crossing the continent lay in more than that and it only dawned on me at that moment.

I thought of my parents and how difficult it would be for them to accept. The dream of the rich Irish farmer with the land was slowly slipping away for my father anyway, but this would really be a major hit! I thought of the future and the cultural, societal barriers that would have to be knocked down. Would he ever be able to take me for dinner? What presents would I ever get for Christmas? These questions surprised me. I hadn't realised this shallow nature lay inside of me, how strong my cultural conditioning was, how much of a victim of my own Culture I had become. But they were questions and they obviously meant something to me if I was asking them now. Instead of being hard on myself for allowing them to surface, I allowed them to take their course. If I was to choose to be with this man, I had to let go of so many things. I had to get rid of the dream of marrying a rich man with a big house. That was the easy way out. What kind of life would we have? He wasn't qualified in any academic subject, how would we get by? As these questions overwhelmed my consciousness, I began to break them down. The biggest question for me was 'How much value do I put on money and things compared with love?'

I knew then that whether he was rich or poor, dripping in letters after his name or not, it was much more important to me that he was a good man and that I loved him.

How would my community feel about me with a black man? The race card was pulled in the corners of my mind and I questioned how we would be perceived. I had to question my own stance on race. It meant facing my colour head on. As a white person, did I feel superior in some way, would I come to resent him in life for his colour? I wasn't sure if I really felt like that as I had never thought about it before and even if traces of that existed within me, he would help me fight them. I had never cared much for the judgements inflicted by others so I would not start now. If anyone had an opinion about us or our circumstances, then it was up to them to question themselves.

As I had gone through before, there was the visa, the distance, religion and practical issues to contend with but, for now, I was making a decision.

I knew now that with the decision I made, I would be choosing to deal with consequences of that choice.

The prospect of returning home, looking around for the 'right man' didn't particularly appeal to me. It led me to question what I actually believed to be the right one. I had never believed that there was one person for each of us. That was just a myth to justify people leaving perfectly adequate partners when the going gets tough so they can drift into other relationships in hope that this person will be perfect. It is ridiculous when we think about it. To look at the society we live in for a moment. In a world of mass separation, incessant adultery, multiple divorces, it is only right to question the philosophy of 'the right one'. All of these unfortunate situations occur because people go into relationships and marriages expecting this person to be right for them. They may accept certain flaws in their loved one but when the 'flaw' is exacerbated into constant conflict, people tend to come to a realisation that this person may not be the one they thought would be perfect for them. The reality dawns like a dark cloud encapsulating them and then the only 'logical' solution comes into play which is to leave and find a person who does suit. The problem lies in this. If we really believe that the person is out there and that he or she is perfect, we could be waiting our whole lives, running from one relationship to another hoping it doesn't get tough and praying that we no longer have to run.

How about accepting that the perfect person does not exist and we must choose to love someone we would like to spend our time with and who we love so much.

I was left with this train of thought penetrating the inner working of my mind, flowing into my veins making me shiver with fear and excitement. I loved this man and, even though there may be someone greater for me out there, I was going to choose him and if it gets tough I will try with all the power in me to make it work and stick it out.

For now, I had to get on with my visit to the village and hold on to my decision until I returned to his village that evening.

In this new village, it appeared that the chief had called a meeting with me having heard of the school project, to request a similar development in his community.

The ritual began with me sitting among the elders, speaking to the Chief and his translator. It was a pleasant encounter which led to the Chief himself giving me a tour of the village. The school was very basic and was in desperate need of renovation. Some of the children were under a tree learning maths and it was heart breaking. It is important to remember at times like this that I was not here to save Ghana in any way and that my small contribution to the project we had invested in was through personal interest more than anything. People needed financial help and I was in a position to assist. I knew these people because this small village was in close proximity to the place I had lived and the school I had worked in. I knew there was a limit on what I could do. I had to keep my head in reality. I would love to have millions and I would love to think that I would use my wealth to help those in need but for now, it was a very small contribution for one school.

I explained all of this to the Chief but he seemed to think that I would return one day with the money and help the community. I made no promises but that we all live in hope. His dazzling gold ring and chains distracted me from my usual sympathetic ear and I was so close to asking him to sell one of them to build a school that I hardly listened to much of the pitch. It was always difficult for me at these times to understand the relationship between the Chief and the community but this man genuinely showed concern for the people. His wealth was a factor which allowed his position to exist and I accepted that as I accept that Ireland's Taoiseach gets paid more that the President of the United States of America. I sometimes complain about it but generally it doesn't affect me.

I was given fufu to eat and it was the most delicious meal I had had in Ghana. The soup was so spicy that it made steam stream from my ears but I was becoming accustomed to this level of heat by now and enjoying it more and more all the time. I just looked ridiculous to everyone else, especially as my faced turned the colour of a tomato and my nose was running profusely!

After washing it down with a cold malt, we headed back on the tro tro for a long journey to a more familiar place.

As soon as I arrived back home to Oda, I went to the market where I knew he would be. We began our walk which we would often have in the evenings stopping off at a 'spot' (which is what they call bars—being an open space with some plastic chairs, an array of local brew and some

Star beer!) to sit and continue the epic conversation which that day had brought.

He knew I was acting strange but as it is not in the nature to ask whether I was ok or not, I eventually said I had something to say. Being the insecure analytic woman my sex expects me to be, I firstly just want to confirm that he had strong feelings for me even though I knew the answer as I he had been saying it up to now. He didn't really understand this I idea of wanting to reaffirm thongs all the time. Anyway, he believed that he loved me and if there was any possibility, he would spend his life with me, either in Ireland or here in Ghana. I told him the thoughts that had consumed me on the journey and the conclusion I had come to. I wasn't going home to keep looking for something that I may or may not find. Instead I accepted that I loved him and I wanted to spend my life with him too. I had so many questions to go through about the future, the difficulties, how to tell our families but suddenly, none of that mattered. In the moment, we knew it was right and that was all that we were concerned about.

Now, the fun would begin but not before the evening by the river. When 2 people have so many things to consider before they can be together, a certain level of commitment is needed to really be sure that it will move ahead. I knew that I was aware of this but when we sat by the river and I saw a shining ring coming my way, it was still scary!

He told me he would love me for the rest of my life and I think he asked me to marry him, or at least it was implied. I don't really remember as I was shaking like a leaf.

Among the euphoria, a sense of overwhelming guilt and anxiety set in.

The race to acceptance had set off and my flight home was a week away. I would hold it in until then and then drop the bombshell.

CHAPTER 12

BUILDING THE BRIDGE

It was all getting too familiar. Leaving this country, saying Goodbye, packing my summer clothes away and taking out the jeans ready for landing in Dublin. This time, somehow, I knew I would see everyone again very soon in the future. One in particular!

I set out for Katoka airport not really sure what was going to happen next. I had a ring on my finger, love in my heart but no idea when or where this 'wedding' would ever take place.

My thoughts shifted towards my family and friends and as we soared back over the Sahara towards Europe, my nerves began to take over.

It is an amazing mixed feeling when you let go of a life planned for yourself and embrace something unknown. I hadn't realised until that trip what I actually wanted in my life and most of it stemmed from fairy tales told to me by my parents in hope that I would one day be the princess of the story. I was so far from those fairy tales now, head up in the clouds, in love with a country I had not known existed a few years before, in love with a man I didn't know a whole lot about. Sometimes, getting lost in life, losing your way can open so many more opportunities. When we are lost, we open our eyes to find the way and see so much more. When we are fixated on one thing and we strive to go towards that we can miss what goes on around us, miss seeing people, following other options. On a road less travelled, the world can seem so much more intriguing.

Tearing away layers of a life we believe is for us is not easy and it involves pain and anxiety but with the falling of each layer comes relief, greater understanding and a glimpse of enlightenment.

The first challenge is to dispel the image of happiness parents hold for us. The fairytale is not something created in our own imagination but dreams held by those in authority who love us so that we can be happy by conforming to a society that isolates those who are different.

I hadn't set out to act differently, I had just kept an open mind and heart and allowed so many things that were unfamiliar to me to become part of my life.

I hoped everyone would understand.

When we landed at Dublin, I came out glowing with mixed emotions and happy to be back home knowing that I was committed to a Ghanaian and that he and Ghana were now part of my life.

My sister was the first to see the ring and it was great that she was so happy for me and smiled when she figured it out. I will always appreciate that reaction from her and I don't think she ever realised how much. Then I watched my mother's face drop as I told her I had decided to marry a man she had never met and was from a world where she donates money to every now and again. She hugged me and told me she would support me no matter what but I should think it through as he could be after anything. She had many mixed emotions too and I think she just wanted to tell me that I was a silly girl with my head in the clouds but, as she is such a wonderful supportive person, she held it in.

That, along with pure silence from my Father was what I generally received upon delivering the news. My father is a man who enjoys talking and for him to be so silent said it all to me. My friends wanted to know how culturally we would work. We would laugh later on thinking of the first question to be asked; 'Does he drink?' I think they were worried of his social behaviour not fitting into a world of heavy drinking sessions and hangovers from hell. I assured them that he was Christian (as I knew that they were thinking about movies such as 'Not Without My Daughter' where women are whisked away after the wedding to become slaves for the men') and that he had no intention of holding me prisoner after the wedding or using me to enter the country. He had social graces, bone chewing and spitting aside, and would be able to blend into Irish society should we decide to live there. This was another factor. I believe people were worried that I might up and disappear to Ghana forever but I knew we would try to work in Ireland as the work I did in Ghana was voluntary and I would need to make money if I was ever to return again.

I convinced my family that I had thought it through but I knew they also needed time to unravel the layers of cultural conditioning and I knew they would need to meet him to believe that he truly was a 'proper suitor'. It was not conventional in any way but my father could see that conventionality had not proved too successful for the thousands of divorcees in Ireland. Race marrying race did not mean automatic happiness and suitability. There was no guarantee that I was ever going to meet anyone, let alone somebody who would treat me as Kwabena did. I could see in my fathers' eyes that these conversations were carrying weight but time would be needed to truly understand as it had taken me and as it would continue to take me.

My sisters and brothers were excited at the prospect of a new face in the family, a new race that they could teach their children about and learn about themselves. It inspired curiosity in most people.

Then, there was the walking on egg shells as everyone tried to avoid the inevitable race-related vocabulary. My mother would apologise after saying that she should take out the 'black bag'!

'Sorry, I didn't mean to offend', she said but I had no concern given that the bag was in fact black in colour! Every time the words 'black' or 'Africa' were mentioned, everyone looked in my direction awaiting a reaction. I understood and even when the racist comments would come later I always remembered advice from some Ghanaians. Racism is the problem of the racists, not our problem. Those words always allowed me to hold my head up high. My family was worried because they knew it would be difficult in Ireland to walk hand in hand with a black man and not expect people to stare or criticise. I knew my country to some extent, but it was true that I had no idea of how people would react. I did know, however, that I could control my own reactions and this is what I would have to do. I had to prepare for reactions, both negative and ignorant and try to let go. Most people are not nasty or vindictive in Ireland but we simply were still not used to 'foreigners'. It was not like the streets of London, or other European cities were the overflowing melting pot spilled onto the minds of the natives. We had not really had to ask ourselves questions about how we felt about non-nationals setting up home in our country. We thought it was temporary, or it wouldn't affect us as long as our children didn't marry into the foreign culture. We would be polite, mostly tolerant, but we didn't have to make friends. Now I myself and my family were in a position where we could no longer remain detached and distant but to embrace the joining of other cultures and customs.

Suddenly, we found ourselves taking interest in the Nigerian family living near my sister, or the black guy who works in the local supermarket. We were watching programmes about people volunteering in African countries, the cocoa plant in Ghana, immigration and everything else that was now relevant. It is amazing how so much in the world is redundant to us; how irrelevant so much of what we see and hear is. It is equally as fascinating to think how it becomes our focus as soon as something in our life changes. This is how clear it is that our lives can sometimes become monotonous. We go about our daily routine. That is not monotonous in itself as our routine can be fulfilling to us. It is that everything we associate with our lives remains in the same realm. We do not deviate from what we see as relevant. We watch the same soap operas as that is what they talk about in our workplaces. We read the same newspapers and magazines so we know the same information as most other people. We go to the same bars and restaurants and if we have never heard of the latest 'celebrity', our peers wonder what stone we have been living under. When we travel down the less travelled path, we discover a whole other world out there with people suffering, people living in happy, peaceful places. We step outside the bubble and open our eyes. We know more than the latest story in a soap opera like *Coronation Street* and other things become relevant.

I observed this passage within my own circle and it was wonderful to see.

However, I needed to get my fiancé to Ireland to meet everyone before the wedding. It would be completely unorthodox to walk up the aisle with someone my own mother has never had a chance to criticise or my friends have never weighed up!

We started the ball rolling with the documentation needed to acquire a visitor's visa to Ireland. We put in the application from the charity angle, which we had set up in Ireland but with activity based in Ghana led by my fiancé. We hoped the immigration office would see his coming to Ireland as a bridge between the two countries. I organised a letter of invitation, got all my financial records together along with references and anything else I thought might convince the office that I would support as man who wasn't coming to suck the government of resources or to traffic African women.

Unfortunately, on the dusty continent, my fiancé had applied stating that we were intimately connected. Of course, this was true and I never denied it in the application but I was inexperienced at this type of thing and I felt that the business route would be far easier. We talked every day but neglected to mention that we had different information on our applications! We almost didn't want to discuss it—the African elephant in the room. We thought if we buried our head, it would pass over us and be alright in the end.

I grew up in the Irish Bertie years of the roaring Celtic Tiger where everything was available to me. One of the Pope's children, guilty of indulgence despite the price tag, the distance or the consequences. ('The Pope's children' is a term given to people in Ireland conceived at the time Pope John Paul visited in 1979 who want it all and want it now!)It is not the same as being spoilt in the sense of the child stamping their feet. The Tiger bore a different type of spoiled children. Parents submitted because they had the money. So, we, later in life gave in to our own desires. If we couldn't pay for it now, the credit card would. These are families who were not rich. My own family came from humble beginnings but the SSIA savings phenomenon where the government would give you 1 Euro for every 4 you saved, the increased benefit taxes, college grants and other needless outgoings led to a new form of working class. People who did not have to go without. Life seemed so easy when it came to achieving things—the year in Australia, the South East Asia trip, the iPod, the laptop, the car. Although there were pressures in other senses, people didn't really say 'no' in my generation in Europe.

Now, facing another challenge, I believed luck would prevail and these people would agree that we were deserving of a few months together. Needless to say, after 2 months of waiting and hoping, the application was rejected. It was a hard pill for me to swallow. It was much less tough for him in a land where rejection rings through and becomes a way of life. A country where getting money from a bank is like blood from a stone and where you certainly do not get €1 for every €4!

Although I knew that their reasons were perfectly acceptable, it seemed so unfair that your nationality can determine what countries you can take holidays in. Apart from my irrational spoiled cub thoughts, I genuinely was angry at the imbalance spread across the world we lived in.

Couldn't we all travel wherever we saw fit if we wanted to take 2 weeks to escape the madness? We could enjoy 2 weeks safari in Tanzania, climb to Machu Pichu, make a wish at the wall of Israel or even eat some chow mein in the communist world of China.

However, if you were a person who happened to be born to an African mother, there was no way you could decide where to go, pack your bikini and set off. The immigration officers of the western world are the only people in the world who are trained to treat people as guilty before proven innocent. I know it is a tough job and I would hate to be in a position to make those decisions in a world where we strive to protect our cultural identity and, at the same time, push to open our borders so we can live in freedom. We love to speak of meeting new people, welcoming identities but the idea of threatening our jobs or 'taking our women' leads to the controversial discourse of immigration and all the issues it brings. My level of understanding on the issue was always fairly clear. I had studied the area of intercultural and immigration issues and I knew that we couldn't allow the very identity that attracted people to our country to become obsolete and that nation to resemble the very country people run from. However, now I found myself full of anger and resentment at a system that discriminated against the colour of someone's skin. They were keeping us apart, keeping my family from meeting the man I was going to marry. It took me 5 minutes to get my visa for Ghana as they knew I would return home but it would never be imagined that Africans would want to go home. It hurt badly.

The rejection letter listed so many things that we had done incorrectly. It showed how wet behind the ears we were. I had no idea how to get him into the country and I didn't want us to marry so quickly just for the sake of a visa. I had to prepare myself and my family needed time too.

We appealed the decision, sent some photographs but to no avail. We were told we had inconsistencies in our application, there was no evidence that his job would still be there when he returned to Ghana.

His bank account was not active enough. This would be enough to prevent many Africans from coming to Europe.

It was useless. We had to face it that he would never get to Ireland on anything other than a spousal visa.

I was due to go back over for 2 weeks before Christmas and we would make decisions then.

CHAPTER 13

THE NEXT STEP

I returned to Ghana in November for a few weeks to spend some quality time with my fiancé and to decide on the next move. We accepted that he would not get to Ireland on anything less that a spouse visa. We both thought about getting married quickly in a registry office but we decided we wanted it to be a big event and invite our families. I hoped someone would accompany me on the day from Ireland so I had to hope for the best. We lay in each others arms on the Saturday morning and set the date. May 29th. It was official. I would go home, prepare myself emotionally and help to prepare my family. He would organise everything (after speaking to me by phone regarding major decisions).

We would have a big wedding but keep the cost as low as possible.

I chose the venue and church before I left and, as I kissed him Goodbye, I knew my life was suddenly changing at a greater and faster rate. I had a lot of thinking to do. Was I willing to accept that this would not be the fairy tale wedding little girls dream of? We were entering into a term, mostly used by the Americans, called 'miscegenation'. It is not necessarily a negative concept but marrying outside my race was not the image I had when I pictured myself walking down the aisle while I had my pillow case around my head as a veil. However, it seemed so natural now that I was aware of the important things in life. These questions could have alluded me but I chose to allow them to sit for a while so that I could always tell myself I had battled the demons that confronted me. I had fought with the devil's temptation to choose the easy route and miss out on a life with this man. I had the same questions as others would ask when they questioned my motives in my country. I was not defeated by them. I continued to allow terrible things to enter my head so that I was no longer afraid of what the world would throw at me. Would I have to follow the concept of giving up one culture to take on another or would I be able for both of them? None of the questions really penetrated my mind as I knew that the one that mattered had been dealt with.

One of the scariest things about the whole experience was *how* normal it actually did feel. I worried that perhaps, one day when I least expected it, all of this would haunt me. I would realise that this was crazy, find myself a nice Irish man and snap out of this. It seemed right, like this was something I was supposed to do. I have always wondered if we have a purpose to fulfil on this earth. I was not at all sure of what that purpose was, but I felt I was on the right track. I had never really understood why I chose Ghana as the place to go or why I was at all interested in 'volunteerism'. I didn't particularly support the idea of it; the idea of people going over to countries to 'help' in situations where they had no qualifications or experience. Just when the children were getting comfortable, they would leave and never return. I always felt bad about my own experience. Even though I was qualified and experienced, I still left after a few months, having fulfilled my own goals. As I was older and more mature than the average volunteer, I realised this mistake and tried to make up for it by supporting the school over the years, visiting always and providing as many resources as possible. It still doesn't replace the fact that my time would have been much better spent staying on to see the children do exams. It made me wonder why I had ended up there.

When I was planning my wedding from Dublin to this man in Ghana, it all made more sense. I would always have a connection to the country, to the people. They would teach me so much and I would teach them. I would marry into the culture and a bridge would be built.

During the preparations, I was asked if I was marrying him for love of him or the country. I had to ask myself my true intentions. I did love the country but deep down I pictured us living in other countries and I still saw happiness. He was special and I loved him. There was no question of dubitation that came my way. I found myself with an answer to everything, but not in defence. If I had to defend it, then I wouldn't be sure myself. No, I just knew what I was doing.

While I was initially preparing my mind, I obviously informed my family of the big day. I announced in a way that expressed it would be a relatively small event and I understood the distance and the cost made it impossible for people to attend. I really, honestly, without a shadow of a doubt did not expect what came next.

They wanted to be there!! Not only did they want to be there but they were going to make it happen.

I could only imagine how wonderful it would be to have them in my adoptive homeland of Ghana! I didn't quite believe it but, suddenly, people were booking flights and buying dresses. Dreams would come true here. My parents, in their 70s, were getting themselves ready for the trip of a life time. The furthest they had travelled before this time was London and flying was not at the top of my father's bucket list!!

Meanwhile in Ghana, the preparations were getting under way. Any woman reading this will find it difficult to imagine allowing the man to organise the entire wedding. It was something I had resigned myself to when I decided to marry a Ghanaian. I would get my dress at home, organise the logistics for everyone travelling to the wedding and I would make most of the decisions about what was happening there!

My fiancé would call me when the colour of the flowers were being decided, or the cars were being picked and especially when it came to the food and alcohol.

I had been to weddings in Ghana and they were very different to Irish weddings so it was difficult for me at the beginning to let go of the 'dream' wedding. Fortunately I had never planned a big wedding in an expensive hotel so I was never sure of what was in store for me. But now that I was faced with the prospect of an African wedding, I found myself grieving the loss of something that must have been resting in my culturally conditioned mind. I had always said I wouldn't like a 'big' wedding, but now that my turn had come around, I changed my mind! I wanted it to be huge. It would be a combination of African and Irish—an usual combination, a setting of 2 cultures coming together historically in a small village in Ghana. Everyone from the village and all surrounding villages would want to be there. It had to be big!

We set out with a relatively big budget (miniscule compared to the average Irish wedding) and prepared for the royal Ghanaian wedding of the year. I almost expected 'Hello' or 'OK' to call me by the time we had finished.

We decided that the theme would be the tricolour so he organised the men's suit to have white shirts, green ties and orange flowers in the pocket. The thought of the green flowers had disturbed me but my fiancé was adamant so I let that decision pass and hoped for the best. The church would be decorated in green, white and orange and the cake would be done the same way.

As the minor details were being attended to, I had one major issue to contend with. The religious divide had never been an issue in the relationship apart from when I had to inform my Catholic family. But now, we were faced with the decision of what church to get married in. Traditionally, both in Ireland and Ghana, the woman gets to choose the church. The wedding day is all about want she wants and how she wants it done. It seems that this is the general consensus world over.

I just wasn't comfortable that my Presbyterian fiancé, who had attended church all his life, would now have to spend time working with the catholic priest when I wasn't even around. We decided it would be easier all round if we got married in the Presbyterian church and then had a Catholic blessing when he moved to Ireland. My limited involvement in education in the village had been in the local Presby school so I was also more familiar with the pastors and congregation.

Little did I know how difficult this decision would be from the point of view of the Catholic Church. I wanted everything to be done properly so that years down the line, there wouldn't be any problems with children going to schools or within the faith that I had lived by ever since my birth. I felt I owed it to my identity to respect that I was Catholic and I wanted my marriage recognised by them.

The first move was to ask permission from the Archbishop of Dublin. I would require permission for marrying out side of my church and a dispensation for marrying out of my religion. I wrote a very nicely worded letter to the office of the Archbishop and, with the help of my parish priest, set up some meetings. Over the following weeks, I received many calls from the office and I was pleasantly surprised by the reaction I got. Among all the chaos, negativity and downright disaster that had become the Catholic Church in Ireland, I found them very helpful, open to my situation and they were happy to grant the dispensation based on the fact that I clearly loved this man and that our children would be brought up as Catholics. We have a tendency to become defined by certain aspects of our surroundings. In many ways, I found this throughout the process of this religious 'classification'. I had never really questioned my loyalty to a religion I was automatically brought up into. It had always seemed normal to attend mass on Sundays, say the angelus before the news and celebrate the various holy days recognised within my faith. But truly, when you look deep inside the philosophy which drives Catholicism, are we really following it in a pious, obedient manner? Are we to choose parts of it which we agree with and ignore the aspects which we can justifiably reject? We can baptise our children as that is the catholic thing to do but we think the church's stance on contraception and homosexuality is outdated and ridiculous. I don't think it is suppose to work like that. We are supposed to take all or nothing. I wondered about these questions as I went through this process and it turns out I am not so tolerant of the religion I grew up in. My belief in God and love would stand to me whatever church I was part of and I would always respect my church, but I was allowing any guilt in making the decision to spend much of my life between different faiths.

As part of the process, I would have to have a Catholic Priest at our wedding in Ghana who would fill out a dispensation form after the wedding. This, along with the one filled out by my priest, would be kept on file in my parish and would mean the marriage is fully recognised by the church. I was happy with that. It made it all seem more 'acceptable' somehow.

Back in Ghana, I had no idea what was going on with the church. I had picked out a beautiful Presbyterian church as the dream wedding venue but somehow some American who had ancestors in Ghana and wanted to marry a Ghanaian had booked it before us for that date. So I was told to wait for the surprise. There was another church I had never seen which was reserved for our day. The surprises kept coming and the more they did, the less controlling I felt. It was good, I suppose. When everything goes to plan and then something small collapses, the world around you can collapse with it.

However, as everything was falling into place, I did feel more and more anxious. It wasn't so much the details of the wedding preparation but just whether the whole thing would ever come to fruition.

I had chosen my bridesmaids and we set about trying on the greenest dresses in Dublin we could find. The accommodation was all booked, bags were getting packed and even the documents were coming together.

The immigration solicitor had put together a mammoth of a case for us. She believed that on this occasion, after the wedding, there would be no reason for the visa to be refused. I had written a 4 page letter explaining our lack of experience previously, describing our relationship background and outlining the wedding plans. The fact that my own parents would be witnesses would definitely boost the chances in this case. We would just need to add the marriage certificate and the photographs to it. The package destined for the UK and Ireland embassy in Ghana contained:

1. A full relationship history, written by myself, dating back to the first glimpse at the wedding all those years ago. (Thank God I kept diaries!!)
2. Bank statement from the previous 6 months from his Ghanaian account and my account in Ireland.
3. Savings details showing sufficient funds to host my husband in Ireland and cover any emergency expenses.
4. A letter from my landlady stating that Kwabena could live at the address upon entry.
5. The dispensation letter from the Catholic church (not essential but the solicitor thought that this showed dedication to the marriage)
6. Photographs of us from different stages of the relationship.
7. Copies of our passports.
8. A letter from my employer stating that I was in full employment.
9. A police clearance for him.
10. Medical report for him.

It looked complete and with the certificate and wedding photos added, it seemed we had ticked all the boxes. I would now forget about this aspect of the marriage and deal with it during the waiting period which would follow after the wedding. For now, there was too much to do.

As everything was coming together, there was one cloud hanging over our heads—literally. The Icelandic volcanic ash cloud threatened to destroy our chances of flying that week. A volcano called Eyjafjallajokull had erupted in Iceland preventing flights from passing across much of Europe. What are the chances?

The tension loomed as I watched the news everyday and, for the first time in my life, I was obsessively concerned with the direction of the wind. I followed the weather reports meticulously, wind changes and everything else in the world of Meteorology.

For some reason, a particular airline decided to strike at the same time so it seemed the logistics of transferring 4 groups of people on different flights as well as myself and the wedding dress (as one entity) were getting more and more out of my reach.

My fiancé, as always, had the utmost faith and believed that this wedding would go ahead no matter what. I had to trust that he was right and we continued as normal to make arrangements for injections for the family, loads of sun cream as they all believed they were going to fry under the heat of the African sun. My mother referred to all the images of death and suffering she had been exposed to in the western media and began to feel nervous. She was particularly concerned by the heat as years of menopausal flushes came back to haunt her. I could see by her that she felt this journey may be the death of her!

I was given 16 passports which I brought to the Ghana Consulate in Dublin and had them all stamped and processed in 20 minutes.

The morning I was due to leave, the cloud of ash had passed and left only a cloud of anticipation. I took the flight . . . . my last as a single woman!

CHAPTER 14

LAST MINUTE PLANS

I arrived a week before the big day and saw, once again, that man I would spend the rest of my life with. Not a cold foot did I feel.

That evening, I remembered what had brought me to this corner of the earth 2 years ago. I sat with a local of the village discussing the 'meaning of life'. Sitting with this woman discussing the daily struggle brings me back to that humble feeling that I had acquired in abundance during my visits to this country. Recently, I had been preoccupied with my own goals, but as always, we are given reminders in different forms of what is really important. I asked her what she meant by her 'daily struggle'. Her ultimate reason not to panic was her pure faith in God. We spoke of a passage from the book of Daniel in the bible. What had always been a story read to me when I was young suddenly became illuminated there and then. Daniel had been thrown into the Lion's Den for his resistance to the law forbidding people to pray to God. After he is thrown in, he shows no sign of despair or panic. Despite what is facing him, his belief in the power of God and the knowledge that He exists is enough for him to remain calm in the face of diversity. Imagine if we all had this sense of reassurance where we didn't have to panic or worry when something bad was happening in our lives. It would save so much pain and anguish in the world. This woman is a devout Christian and her ability to love and smile comes from her faith. I ask her a question that always follows me around in this journey in the world. Why is it that God allows them to suffer so even though they practice the word of the Bible? She tells me that for all the love God gives, Satan provides an equal amount of pain and suffering to counteract it. It is so hard to imagine that this woman, so full of life, is below the poverty line. She describes how she thinks our cultures are different and thinks it is important as I am about to marry a man with similar values to her. My ears are wide open! I really had no idea of what I was doing!

When a person's brother, sister, or any relative is sick, it is up to the person in the family with the most money at that given time to assist. (She informs me that she is aware we Westerners have an establishment called 'a home' where we tend to send our sick and elderly. It is a phenomenon far removed from these people who see the individualism that rules our society is detrimental to our spiritual growth. There is also a soft awareness that this 'individualism' allows us to grow economically and financially on the other hand.)

If that relative in question then dies, the financial burden then turns to much more than that. That person inherits the children of the dead and must provide for them until they are old enough to fend for themselves. There are times when this is seen as an investment if the children grow up educated and bring money back to the family. The possibilities of this lie in the following situations:

- A rich uncle unknown to most people returns from the USA or Europe and distributes a fortune among his long lost family.
- A scholarship is granted on the basis that the child is highly intelligent, receives excellent results and is brought on by a teacher who is willing to pursue the cause.
- They meet and marry someone rich.
- Enough money is raised to send the child or children abroad with the intention of sending back enough dollars or Euros to look after the family in their old age or returning from abroad with an education great enough to earn huge money in Ghana.

Some of the above do happen but not often enough. They are the exceptions but usually the ones we hear about. The Michael Essiens of this world. (Essien is a professional footballer who plays for Ghana and Chelsea at that time)

So, in Ghana, this woman represents a large proportion of the struggling population. She recognises, however, that they struggle less than other countries around them in this continent.

She has 2 children of her own and 2 from a sister who died a few years back. She had paid for some of the medicine and now is responsible for the children. While these children are her nephews, they are immediately referred to as her children. Her sister's husband visits sometimes but works in the capital mostly contributing very little. Her own husband left for work one day and has never returned. Her means of income is selling what she can as most women do in Ghana. She may take in 3 to 5 Ghana cedi a day (€1.50 to €3.50) which keeps food on the table and a roof over their heads. This would be sufficient, but unfortunately her sister has no work and her mother is ill so she has many to provide for. With no prospects of a loan, winning money or social welfare, it is extremely difficult for her. But she doesn't panic. Bitter sweet African life.

Having listened to Emilia, I thought about how I would be pulled in life. I wanted to be comfortable, but I knew when I entered this marriage, I would also be responsible for assisting my husband's relatives here. We would always be better off because we had access to credit and welfare. It would be something to get used to but I liked the idea that we could help. Did I want to inherit a load of kids? There was a possibility that I would not have children myself after a series of tests and procedures on my ovaries stemming from the unfortunate presence of something called polycystic ovary syndrome. Perhaps, it would be a way of bestowing us with children. Who knows?

Well, there would be give and take and this would be a time when I may or may not be quite so tolerant of my partner's custom! I would, however, accept whatever would be put in our path. I had chosen that and I would live with it.

It was Wednesday of the week of the wedding. The wedding was on Saturday and the Irish guests would be arriving in the country from today. It was all quite surreal. The bridesmaids were first to arrive and I got my first 'oohhh, he is gorgeous' from the girls!

I had now gone from being the clueless little white girl to the tour guide and I suddenly found myself knowing more than I thought. It was at that point I realised I could put this book together. I had been consciously and subconsciously taking things in.

The girls were impressed by the landscape and immediately warmed to my fiancé. I was delighted with this. It was too late to go back now, but we all need approval from those we are closest to. I hadn't realised how important this approval was until I got it. It was sealing my faith in my own decision. I needed others to see that I had met a good man. I just hoped my parents and family would react similarly. It wouldn't be that I would run from him without the approval of my loved ones as my journey belongs to me and I had struggled to decide this one but it would mean life would be marred by the disapproval and worry from those around us. Thankfully, this wasn't to be the case.

We had a great evening. We drank beers and talked for hours. This was a breath of fresh air for my friends as part of them still thought this was madness. But sitting there, doing what we do at home, gave them comfort that maybe I wasn't completely out of my mind. It all seemed very 'normal'. They questioned his motives and I suspected they had decided on the way over that they had to make sure this guy was genuine and that they would iron out any issues they had with him before the wedding!

116

The next evening marked the arrival of the O'Connor family. 3 different planes would land in the course of the evening and the clan would be on them (hopefully) dying to meet the mystery black man that had stolen their little girl's heart and caused so much disruption and excitement.

The brothers and sisters came first and the hugs, kisses and questions began flying as soon as possible.

I saw my parents from outside the terminal when they first came off the plane. I was so blessed to have them here and proud that they had cared enough to come all of this way both to wish me the best and to inform me as to whether I was doing the right thing or not.

The first introduction to my fiancé was marred with some complications.

There was a massive thunderstorm the night they arrived and the rain poured down from imaginary buckets, lightening lit up the whole sky and the thunderous roars were haunting. My mother had had her hair done beautifully to make an impression on her new son-in-law but when she stepped onto the African soil, the monsoon rain flattened it leaving the styling unrecognisable. This upset her and the first thing she said to Kwabena was 'I am so sorry about my hair, I tried to keep it nice but the rain has destroyed it'. He was not as concerned by her hair as she might have thought!!

My father, who is afraid of flying, had to be pumped full of Whiskey and valuum just to get him to make the journey. When he arrived, he thought everything was 'wonderful, brilliant'. He hardly noticed that his future son was black even though he had been struggling with the whole thing for the last couple of years. It was so funny and we would all laugh later at the hilarious scene at the airport.

We plied everyone into a van and set off on the dusty, wet roads of Accra. From the very first journey, everyone was pleasantly surprised by this country they had heard so much about. Looking out the window,

I saw my mother's fascination with a land she had always dreamed of visiting in her lifetime. She watched the bustling market stalls on the side of the streets selling oranges and meat. They were lit up by candles designed to keep the dreaded mosquitoes away. There was a surprise at the amount of large buildings, recognisable companies and abundance of shops. It was good in a way that they had met with the capital first as the village would be quite a different story.

We all left the bags at the hotel and went for a drink to break the ice. When my mother had recovered form the hair crisis and my dad had sobered up, they spoke to Kwabena in length. My mother turned to me and said 'I understand now'. I knew then that she could see what attracted me to this place and this man. I could see my father battle with the skin colour but this was the first time he was forced to see past the black and I knew he was slowly coming to terms with everything and he quickly began to love this man. My parents were amazing. How they adapted to this environment and opened their hearts to the people around them. My future husband was seeing a side to me he had never known. He could see the love I had been part of and it made him respect me more. In Ghana, as in our own culture very often, our families are a great reflection of ourselves. The fact that these people loved me so much to come all the way here enhanced his idea that, perhaps I was a good person to love. Then there was the side to me that he had never really seen in depth. He did begin to see that I talked more than he thought. Quite a lot more actually!

I had always remained relatively quiet in the midst of him and his friends. They often spoke Twi and he watched me observe from corners and make the odd contribution when the conversation went bilingual. Now, he saw that I had so much to say. It would be difficult for him to get used to but something he would have to accept! There would be difficult moments ahead but none we couldn't handle, hopefully.

I left my family to sleep their first night in the deep African darkness and waited for the following day when we would do our last minute visits of in-laws before the wedding.

In the morning, we walked around to the rooms of all the family and friends to see the reaction in the light of day. Everyone was looking cheerful and impressed by the African plains clearly seen outside the windows.

The wedding cars were hired early to take people from Accra to the village and so, we set off for the journey to Oda.

This was the moment when the poverty and lack of infrastructure could really be seen. Accra can be somewhat of a 'disappointment' to those who expect to see the image of Africa. The emaciated children covered in flies are not so prevalent in the thriving capital city and often people feel that they are not seeing what 'they signed up for'. This is a terrible idea really, but I have seen this attitude throughout my time here. However, through the small villages on the stretch up to the Eastern region, there are plenty of images of poor families struggling to sell whatever they can, children who should be at school working hard. Ghana has resources in abundance but it is hard to imagine when you see these villages.

As mentioned in Maathai's book, *The Challenge of Africa*, the Ethiopian economist, Fantu Cheru believes the inability for African to capitalise on their resources lies in the lack of political will, weak institutions, a shortage of skills, too many ties to former colonial powers, inadequate infrastructure, transport and communication networks.

The Ghanaian government needs to address these issues and the new leader in power, John Atta Mills was a great contender to tackle the underlying problems. The leaders in Africa in general have a very similar pattern of behaviour and I see it as no different for Mr. Mills. During the colonial period, many Ghanaians were oppressed by the white powers and, often, when they come to power, they themselves take on this sense of superiority and behave in a similar way. The leader can not see how the people in these villages are suffering. While he is intent on demanding loans and grants from Europe and the U.S, the money is not used wisely. It is invested in programmes but it never really reaches the people on the ground. The money is not used to invest in training of those who could benefit. The money given by countries abroad often creates a dependency. This dependency has kept African nations down for years. Instead of using their resources and talents to develop themselves, they look to the richer nations to provide the funding for already 'white run industries'. The Ghanaians need to feel a sense of empowerment in their own nation. They have the cocoa, the gold, the diamonds, the minerals and, most importantly, the spirit but they also need the motivation to combine them, turn away from foreign investors and build themselves up to a be an inspirational African country. I can always see that potential here but there are so many things that need to be put in place before this 'empowerment' can begin. It needs to start in the leadership of the country. They need to see that, while their faith is a wonderful thing; their faith in God and in foreign countries, it does not need to hold them back. I hope one day, this great country will have the leader it deserves and not someone who looks out for their best interests. Maathai sums up the African leaders very well when referring to a Kenyan farmer who was not familiar with the process of planting on slopes and therefore was not benefiting from the potentially vast supply of trees:

'If the African leaders had invested more in education, the creation of sustainable employment options, and inclusive economies, and if they had been more concerned with the welfare of their people and not their own enrichment, then perhaps this farmer would have gone to school'

It is a deep issue affecting the country, and indeed the continent, and the effects could clearly be seen on this trip to the village.

CHAPTER 15

MEETINGS AND GREETINGS

We arrived at the hotel which would be the setting for the wedding reception. It is so beautiful. Palm trees surrounding the entrance, a swimming pool (well, something similar) and a wide open space. It was a beautiful hotel, and while I had never stayed in it before, I always thought it would be a perfect location for a wedding if I was every to get married in Ghana!

My family and friends settled in nicely in their quiet hotel rooms before it was time to hit the chaos of the village market and meet Kwabena's family. His mother had a shop in the market but it seemed every stall, among the goods it sold, held a relative of the family in some form. Now that the wedding was the most exciting thing in town, there were even more relatives coming from all corners to meet 'obruni's' family; 'obruni' being the name for white people. I had not properly prepared the Irish guests for what would come next.

We stepped out of the cars into the main street. Kwabena had gone to sort out some things for the wedding as it was the following day and I was too busy showing off my family and friends to assist so I was left to enter the madness myself.

I lead everyone down a small path into the market and, suddenly, the wonderful cries of excitement and joy ran through the entire market. My guests were stunned. All the market women came up to hug them, kiss them, and even lift them off their feet. There were people coming from all angles and it was difficult to bring my mother to Kwabena's mother. They were all saying they were his mother (a typical Ghanaian tradition of friends of a mother becoming the 'mother' of all the children). My mother was completely confused and turned to me on several occasions 'is this his mother?'

Eventually, I found my very soon to be mother-in-law and the two met for the first time.

It was a very emotional moment for me as I watched them hug and exchange words (limited but meaningful). My father was next to greet her but in the Ghanaian matriarchal world, the mother was the most important person around.

Everyone hugged as the shouting got louder. The women in the market had never seen so many white people in one place at one time. The excitement about the historical wedding could be felt all around the village and my guests were overwhelmed to be part of it. I was worried that I couldn't be present, in the moment. I was caught up in making sure everyone was happy and had enough water and sun cream. I tried to let go but I wasn't sure what to do with myself!

We moved through the stalls of dried fish, cosmetics, rice and exotic fruit onto Kwabena's uncle. We greeted him and also Kwabena's sister who worked with him. We then met his brother, some aunts (although I still to this day can't be sure who is his aunt and who is his mother's friend claiming to be his aunt. It took a while to believe who his real mother was!)

I could see at this point my parents were feeling the love a little a too much and the heat was getting to them. It was the first time that they had been exposed to the direct heat of the sun so the air conditioned cars would be a welcomed treat at this stage.

I then took them to meet various people I had known over my time in this familiar place. I know they were surprised by how comfortable I was there. They could see how I had taken to it so much as the people were very similar to me and the lifestyle was something I had always loved.

We visited the school which was in the process of being built with money from the NGO I had set up the previous year. It was coming along nicely and the children who were to benefit from it came up to greet everyone with their little smiles and laughter.

Writing the words makes me realise the whole thing was quite an ego trip for me. I suppose, in a way, it was me showing off. It was all just so exciting to share this part of my life with the people I loved most in the world. I had never imagined that I would be able to and now here they were.

The afternoon was pressing on and I was getting married the next day so people went off their separate ways. Some went walking through the Ghanaian village to witness the buzzing life of its people. Some went back to the hotel room craving the peace that is so difficult to find in most African villages when you are a white person! My parents took a nap and I spent the evening getting my attire ready for the following day.

That evening, we sat around the hotel grounds having a few drinks and discussing the events of the day. It was truly magical. My fiancé arrived back and joined us. I left him early, kissed goodnight and we knew the next time we would see each other was at that alter taking the biggest step of our lives.

It suddenly hit me that I needed my family and friends now as I entered a new realm of my life filled with uncertainty and joy.

A fairly sleepless night followed!

CHAPTER 16

BRIDGING THE GAP

Racial divide is a major issue throughout the world. We live in our bubble identifiable by the colour of our skin, the clothes we wear, our general appearance. The majority of us tend to feel more comfortable with people who look like ourselves. Society is more accepting of people who 'stick to their own'. There is a long history of 'us' and 'them' and there always has to be those who are superior for whatever reason. This leads to someone being inferior so that superiority has weight and can be justified.

It so happens that the white race, being in a geographically ideal position and filled with a desire to have more, greater that any other, became the ones who felt superior. From the Portuguese ships that set sail to conquer Africa for the slave trade, to Columbus 'discovering' the free world to the Roman Empire, these are the people who go down in history as being 'great explorers'. The barbarians were civilised and the world became a greater place. We can think what we like of all this, but the point is, that there is a huge divide evident in the world we live in today. There are those who would believe that white people are somehow 'better' than their black counterparts. History has taught us more than the facts and, unfortunately, if we look deep inside our minds, there is some sense of this.

I woke up on the morning of my wedding and I dug deep inside to bring to the surface any ideas I had about being superior in any way to the man I would marry today. There was a slight tendency in there to revisit earlier issues at why I hadn't 'stuck to my own'. Within a few minutes a flash was pounding in my head reminding me just how much I loved this person and that it was up to us—he and I to accomplish something through this marriage. We would prove to ourselves that the bridge between races could be built and if we could all teach ourselves to be humble, we would never look at another as inferior. I stood in front of the mirror and reminded myself of all the reasons I was doing this and that the most important one, which was love, was still there ringing in my mind like a church bell.

I felt hopeful that my society would accept this as it had many other mixed race relationships and that the world was moving to a place where defining people would become redundant.

I put my ideals to one side and began to focus on the things that any bride would on her wedding day. First task would be to have a glass of champagne, shake off the nerves and get my hair done.

The hairdressers (all 8 of them) came to my room in the morning at 6am. They were responsible for doing the hair of every female in the room and, as they hadn't done white peoples' hair before, the task was not an easy one. Interesting is all I will say but mine looked great and, apparently, that is all that mattered!!

It seems, for a Ghanaian wedding, everyone gathers in the bride's room while she is getting ready. At first, I thought it was wonderful but after a while I needed my space and proceeded to throw everyone out in a horrendous bridezilla manner! This did not go down well later on when I related it to Kwabena!

As is traditional, the best man came to pick me up almost one hour later than the wedding was to start. No panic! This is Africa after all.

I felt a million dollars when I was ready. My father stood next to me proud and emotional. However, in his hazy state still, he did stand on the back of my dress breaking the button to hold the trail up. I just let it wash off me. What can you do?

It was time to go. I was taken through the village like a member of a royal family with people staring and waving in at me and following the car. I waved back out and I remember saying to myself that it was a moment to be cherished

I arrived at the church an hour and a half late and the excitement there was amazing. People had come from near and far to witness this event and the church was so beautifully decorated in the green, white and orange theme. My fiancé had done a great job and his efforts did not go unnoticed by my mother who would always remember how happy he wanted to make me by doing everything so perfectly. She would later say that was how she knew he would be a good husband.

I walked sown the aisle surrounded by familiar and unfamiliar black faces. I saw my white family and friends among them and suddenly it all blended to one. They were all here for the same purpose and they all welcomed the union of 2 people from 2 different backgrounds who were joined by love.

The racial divide all seemed so ridiculous here and now.

I was so comfortable and content walking down that aisle and, as my father handed me over, I looked at my future husband and I felt like I had died and gone to heaven. He looked so handsome and nervous. It was endearing.

He told me I looked beautiful and I weakened like I had met him for the first time.

The service began and it was something to behold. My family would talk about it forever and we had the video to prove to those who couldn't make it.

The pastor preached as if we had all been bold children and now he was setting us straight. He sounded out the abbreviated letters of husband and wife and with each word, we all hung on it dying for more. W.I.F.E represented: wise, industrious, faithful and economical. After each definition, he would look at me for reassurance that I understood.

H.U.S.B.A.N.D represented: humble, understanding, smart, bold, approachable, neat and dutiful. He had a lot more work to do! Our roles as husband and wife were fully addressed and we were made to understand the seriousness of this undertaking. It made me realise that one very significant cultural difference which would be prevalent for us if we lived in Ireland would be this major role divide. At home, duties nowadays are mostly shared as both couples work but not for us. There would be certain tasks where I would be required to attend to and the same for him. While I thought I would come to accept and embrace this defined role idea, it would be difficult for my friends at times when they thought I was being treated unfairly and he should 'get off his lazy arse and do it'. It would be interesting but this was our life to lead and, I can tell you, acceptance is the first secret weapon to maintaining a healthy marriage and, even if we have to learn it the hard way, it proves to be the cement in holding people together,

Almost 2 hours passed and the dancing went on. Everyone, except us, danced around the church. My mother and father looked like they were in a nightclub. It was a scene that nobody would forget. The two families came together through the medium of music and dance and this spiritual moment encapsulated me in a way I had never experienced. The joy in the faces of my family and his. Even now, if I have a low moment, I remember that scene and I feel a sense of joy.

Eventually, the moment arrived to exchange our vows. I looked around the church and I was so happy to have my family there and to see the happiness that this occasion had brought to everyone. Kwabena's father had made a beautiful speech welcoming me to the family, welcoming my family and talking about how this historical moment had brought the 2 worlds together. My father also spoke about how amazing it was but he felt slightly lost for words and this in itself made his words more emotional. I loved him so much for getting up there and showing support.

The vows were also very emotional but it was difficult to shed a tear as the crowd were shouting and laughing as we spoke. There were particular giggles when I pronounced his name in full. It was always funny for an obruni to say anything that resembles Twi but I think they appreciated my effort and their laughter held every bit as much respect as it did mockery. It was another memorable moment of my life.

There it was. We were married. How strange and yet how right.

We made our promises to one another, to God, to everyone there. There was no going back now and we didn't want to go back.

It was only after the vows that I realised one of my bridesmaids had malaria and had spent the whole service outside. I wasn't sure what to do with this at that time but I would have to address it soon after.

The wedding was so extravagant. It could have bordered on tacky if we had had it in Ireland but it was so appropriate as part of the Ghanaian colourful culture. We arrived at the reception and everything was so beautiful. The cake had 6 tiers decorated with bright green fur, orange and white ornaments! I was shocked when I saw it! The tables had statues and fur and the music was blaring as is always the case in a Ghanaian bar.

There were so many people sitting around everywhere looking so glamorous and colourful. The women wore their headscarves and the men were in the best of suits. I didn't recognise some of the faces but I welcomed them all. The bride and groom's family were at the top table and it was all so perfect. There were three white volunteers from Germany who were working in the hospital and had found out about this 'event'. They came along to the wedding on the invite of their host family who, of course, is some distant relation of Kwabena! When the ushers saw them in the crowd, they moved them to the top table, assuming the white folk belonged up there with us!! It was hilarious, I didn't know them at all but I was too relaxed and happy to argue so we accepted them up there and got on with the proceedings.

We danced our first dance just before a giant thunder storm stole the show and the monsoon rain fell on us like a natural hosing.

Kwabena and I decided to dance in the rain as we were determined that nothing would ruin this day. The bridesmaids followed and before we knew it, there were people dancing in the rain around us. I destroyed my beautiful wedding dress and, as my mother was lecturing me on later, I informed her that I didn't plan to wear it again! This was my favourite moment of the day.

The idea of marriage having us in some sort of bondage had crossed my mind, but, at that moment, I felt freer than I ever had. I felt I had made a grown up decision myself and it had lead to this moment. It felt magical. I felt a sense of achievement and pride in everyone there that day. My husband was so handsome and, even though we had destroyed our clothes in the rain, we both felt fantastic.

The day went on and on. The music blasted out African and old pop songs. People danced and the food was in abundance.

The wedding would draw to a close. The honeymoon would begin. Then the marriage would begin. How exactly was that going to go?

CHAPTER 17

—◆◆◆◆—

THE HONEYMOON

It is called the honeymoon period apparently. The glorious time when a couple are first married and everything is so new and exciting. You look your best. You don't want to upset your newly found spouse in the fear that they may think they had a made a mistake. You are funny and sexy with so many interesting things to say. Presumably, this idea comes from the literal honeymoon which is a time of perpetual happiness.

Well, our honeymoon, hopefully, is no reflection of our marriage. Perhaps it was better to start out in life in utter difficulty and be prepared for the hardship of real life.

Firstly, everyone came with us on our honeymoon. We were happy with this as they had all travelled so far for the wedding so it would not have been appropriate to up and leave them in unfamiliar and not so smooth territory so we invited my family and friends to join us for our trip through Ghana. While I had taken a similar journey before where I discovered the different languages, cultures and tribes of the Ghanaian nation, I had never been further than Accra with my new husband.

I know it is all relative—a developed country has a highly developed and functional infrastructure in place and so we complain when the bus is late or if there is a whole in the road. We can't compare our reactions in our country to that of other developing countries. However, it takes time and patience to accept this idea and it doesn't just come the moment you step onto African soil. You don't just have the ability to adapt to the world you find yourself in. I had studied a little bit of anthropology, lived in Ghana and was married to a man who this was second nature to.

However, I had problems sometimes dealing with the environment and the difficulties involved in getting around. And, so, I didn't expect my family or friends to find tolerance placed away in their luggage with their sun cream and mosquito repellent.

The first journey we made took us from the village to Cape Coast. Some family members chose a top class hotel overlooking the sea on the beautiful coast. When we arrived there, our own budget was limited and when Kwabena and I discover they charged their prices in extortionate dollars, we were livid. In true Ghanaian style, we both criticised their policy telling them they were in Ghana and not the United Sates and why were they doing this to people. We realised we were not getting anywhere with this so we left and found ourselves in a much more suitable place, with blood-stained walls from mosquito/human attacks, doors with no handles and the proverbial shower with a bucket and toilet with no flush. We decided, along with my bridesmaids (who were also on a limited budget) that this wasn't quite honeymoon style and we found something in Cape Coast somewhere in the middle of the two.

In Cape Coast, we visited Kakum National Park, walked the suspension bridges and visited the slave castles. Everyone was pretty impressed with the historical tours, the beauty of the Ghanaian coast and the food and hospitality we encountered.

However, it was around this time that the illnesses started to take hold. Already, I had a friend who had malaria. We were not sure at this point what it was but she couldn't hold anything down and we started to get worried. There was another one who had a dodgy stomach and we lost her company for 1 day in the height of the African sun in Cape Coast. Thankfully my parents had left at this time as planned. There was my brother-in-law who took ill also in Cape Coast and a few stories of 'running stomachs' from the others! It became a game of dodging. We were afraid to take certain transport means for fears of not making the journey before toilet requirements reaches an all time high. We had to stay close to places with any kind of a toilet and constant pale sweating and weak faces made it impossible to do certain activities or, indeed, eat certain food.

However, on occasion we had no choice but to carry on. Taking the public transport was indeed a nightmare as people needed to make toilet stops quite often and waiting in those stations became unbearable. I remember one particular trip from Accra to Kumasi (we travelled back to Accra after Cape Coast to make our way up North. The family had left and the friends remained) in which I sat with my very ill friend behind the most disgusting 'toilet' in the world while she wretched in front of our eyes. We decided to take her to hospital in Kumasi. She was given some medication there and released.

There was an opportunity in Kumasi to see the amazing outdoor market which is one of the largest in West Africa. After that, we continued up North to Tamale so that we could show them another side of Ghana and also to visit the Safari in Mole National Park.

The journey to Tamale was difficult as the bus was crowded and the road was particularly bumpy. We were covered in red dust stuck to our skin with the assistance of gallons of sweat which trickled down our bodies. It would take numerous showers to ever be clean again!!

By the end of the trip and as we approached the Muslim-dominated city of Tamale, I could see that releasing my friend from the hospital in Kumasi was a mistake.

We searched for a hotel very quickly, left the luggage and went straight to the nearest hospital. At this stage, she looked like the emaciated version of the girl she once was. It was a scary moment as she collapsed upon entry as if her body had given up. We entered a very nice room almost immediately and it took 10 drips to get the fluid into her body. She was to stay overnight and we would take our turns in sitting with her and not without interesting stories.

The hospital itself was wonderful. I hate to say it, but, here in this developing country, the health service was more efficient than back home. We didn't see people sitting around on trolleys, waiting lists weren't as long as the Great Wall of China and there was enough staff to cover the demand of the patients. She was well looked after and given the correct treatment for her symptoms. Africa is probably the best place to be if you have malaria as they know the disease better than any other. There are countless cases of children and adults diagnosed every day with the disease carried by the most evil insects on planet earth. The females are the culprits—being the only ones to seek out blood for their feed, leaving it digest and then allowing her eggs to develop. The male only feeds on nectar and sugar. If only he could inform his other half that survival is possible without sucking the blood of animals and humans spreading disease and killing thousands of people every day. They say humans are top of the food chain but mosquitoes are certainly giving them a run for their money, especially, in developing countries. Most people suffer from malaria almost every year becoming weak and feverish for a few days or weeks only hoping it doesn't develop into a more serious strand where you find yourself in hospital hoping to hang on to your life. During the wet season, when the sky feels like it is closing in on you and the heat in the air covers you like a duvet, the spread of the disease is fierce. There are no mosquito nets among the natives and babies are constantly at risk.

I always get bitten at this time in Ghana despite my methods of garlic, quinine and every other old wives tale! I took my anti-malaria before leaving each time and I am thankful so far I haven't experienced the wrath of the female vampire.

At some stage in the night, my friend began to feel hungry and I was so excited that she finally desired sustenance. I asked the male nurse on duty for some food or how I could acquire some and he told me to follow him. I did as I was told and before I knew it, I was being led into a car park and toward a small motorbike. He got on and told me to get on behind him. In my short dress, I struggled to get my leg over without flashing all and we were surrounded by locals who taught it was hilarious that this white girl was getting on a bike with a nurse! It never mattered here that you went red with embarrassment. Firstly, you are a different colour no matter what that colour is at any given time and, secondly, the heat made a constant rush of rouge spread across the visage finished with a moist layer of perspiration. One would never be looking one's best but one simply doesn't care!

I was brought to a local bread store after speeding down a main road in Tamale. At this stage I was never surprised by what was going on around me and I always expected something unusual. I colleted the only recognisable things I could find as this was not the time to introduce my friend to the true Ghanaian cuisine that I had come to love so much. She was not a lover of spice at the best of times, so the Ghanaian method of crushing hot chillies into everything would not be appropriate.

I got the most beautiful bread from the bakery along with baked beans and tea. It was a welcome sight for my friend who had not seen any food for days. She was able to eat it and, almost immediately, I watched her perk up and begin to get some life in her cheeks.

When she was discharged, we felt she was well enough (and she felt) to travel to the National park, sit by the pool and watch the wild elephants go by.

The journey to get there was not easy. The bus from Tamale to Larabanga (the town which you need to get to in order to have access to the national Park) was rough. It was so bumpy that you can feel your bones rattling inside you. Your teeth chatter if you keep them together and, if you have a bad back, this is definitely not the place for you. There is no air conditioning and as the road is not in good condition, the bus moves very slowly so having the windows open doesn't particularly help. However, the windows must be left open and, as a consequence, the dirt from the dirt tracks outside comes in leaving all of us white folk looking like orange oompa loompas or girls on a night out covered in that fake tan!

It was really a sight for sore eyes but you just have to laugh. One of the girls was not impressed at all and I could see the desperation to reach our destination in her eyes.

Just when she thought it couldn't get worse . . . .

The bus was packed and, although it never looks like there is more space, the Africans can always make more space. My friend (the displeased one) looked out the window and saw, among many others, a woman holding a live chicken. She commented:

'I hope she doesn't get on here with that thing'.

Not only did the woman get on with 'that thing' but she stood squashed up against my friend. As the bus moved on, the chicken started pecking her on the arm. She became so irritated, I had to take action. We were laughing but we could see she was genuinely afraid and perturbed so I swapped places with her. The chicken didn't touch me. I concluded that he must have sensed her fear and indeed, insults!

My sick friend was doing ok and had a local boy sleep on her shoulder all along the journey. I was so grateful to my friends for joining me in that time of life and, watching them on that bus, I was so proud to have them in my life.

I laughed and chatted to my new husband still in awe at the whole experience and knowing that this wasn't really a test of our marriage but I knew I wanted to know this person better. I loved having him by my side and I wanted so many adventures with him.

We all sat tight and eventually arrived in Larabanga. This is one issue I always have with African countries, and indeed other parts of the developing world. You arrive at a place a few kilometres from a major tourist attraction that takes in lots of money every year but yet there is extreme poverty in the immediate vicinity. Not only does the local area not benefit from the income generated by the tourist attraction, but the development itself upsets the entire surrounding environment. In Ghana in the past food shortages were never a problem. Unlike famine prone countries on the continent, such as Ethiopia and Kenya, Ghana has a climate conducive to mass food production. Even the poorest people in the country had access to fields of plantain and cassava, some even growing at the back of their own dwellings. They may not have had money for many clothes, transport or travel, but at least they would survive and be able to feed their families. That was before the developers came along with the steaming bulldozers and ploughed down land capable of providing food for hundreds. There is no payment in Africa to people who are required to give up their land for construction and so, over the years, the land has been sliced in pieces for the wealthy to build their projects on. This is one major contributing factor to the poverty in Ghana and other parts of Africa. Now, when people are in stark poverty, it can mean having no access to food and starving to death or living in very unhealthy levels of malnutrition.

This town was the doorway for Ghana's most famous safari park but there was no way to get to the park via public transport. We circled the town in the hope of finding some taxi drivers willing to take our large group at a reasonable fee. It was not easy but eventually I found a guy who said he would take us for 100 Cedis!! I almost fell over. €50 for a relatively short journey for 7 people! It was almost Dublin taxi prices!! I informed the man that my husband was Ghanaian and on his way to negotiate. The price immediately started to fall like inflation in a war-torn country. When Kwabena arrived, as always we witnessed the furore of shouting and hand movements which always accompany any civilised Ghanaian business negotiation. In the end, the price went to 20 Cedis which now seemed reasonable but still tourist prices.

We eventually got to the park and I knew everyone would be impressed as I was myself when I first went 3 years before. It is such a beautiful place. It is on the top of a hill and is surrounded by African plains, rivers and we could immediately see the elephants roaming in their own habitat. The pool looked so enticing after the journey we had had but we needed showers before anything else to dispel ourselves of this horrific orange dust firmly based on us by the litres of sweat!

We booked our rooms and my husband and I got a big room to ourselves overlooking the park. It was wonderful. There was finally some honeymoon-like treatment! We took our showers with the buckets of water provided (the park was too far from anywhere to have running water supplied).

The arguments at base were so different from any you could have at home. It wasn't who was wearing whose clothes that caused the girls to dispute, but who had used the most water. This was quite a problem up at the park.

The post-malaria symptoms were still with my friend so, needless to say, she needed water sufficient to flush the toilet on a regular basis. The water was few and far between and did cause disputes but we got there.

We spent the next 3 days in the pool during the day followed by a walking safari and, in the evenings, we would play cards and drink beer.

It was difficult to sleep there with all the insects that were attracted. As we slept, insects would fall on your body one by one. It was too hot to sleep with a blanket so when you look down at your naked body, you see all these black specs of unknown species of insects. Some of them bit so it took some scratching. Some of them were mosquitoes, so you were forced up to spray the room. It is not exactly what honeymoon dreams are made of but we were happy to have this time together so we made the most of it and didn't let the insects in on our honeymoon fun!

At the end of the few days in Mole, it was time to head back towards the capital for everyone to fly home. I think some were relieved. Even though a good time was had by all and the experience was amazing, it can be quite difficult and the comfort of home can be quite appealing by the end.

It was not easy getting back either. There were bumpy dirty rides to be repeated, heated negotiations with taxi drivers, waiting in dodgy bus stations with no toilets, suspicious hotels and various incidents along the way. But, as always, these were overridden by the smiling faces, the colourful people, the laughs from the various sights we witnessed and the magical beauty of the Ghanaian landscape in the background and the Ghanaian will for survival in the foreground. The children who came to us to sell water and other things always made everyone smile, despite the mood. The toilet adventures always kept us entertained as we struggled to find a place that we could go that resembled something more than a hole in the ground.

We would look back at this journey later on and really understand how wonderful it was.

Thankfully, my friend was coming back to her old self and she was enjoying the things she had missed. She was still quite weak and would spend some time in hospital upon return to Ireland also. It would be a long time before she was back to normal but it was a start.

We arrived in Accra and Kwabena and I said goodbye to the Irish crew. I was to stay a few more days both to have some time alone on the honeymoon and to organise the papers we would need to submit for the visa application.

The following days were nice as we were together but we were under pressure to gather everything we could find to accompany the solicitors documents. We had to develop our photographs from the wedding and add the ones we thought were most likely to prove it was all genuine. They all did that. They all looked so beautiful and we were glowing in every picture. There were some with his parents and my parents and we felt this was the best way to go. We should have been putting our album together but, here we were, doing our best to prove our marriage was real. We added some other things that the solicitor had advised including his latest bank statements and some passport photos. We had to photocopy everything as they would ask for this at the embassy.

Finally, it was ready and the day before I was due to return home, we submitted the papers. It was some time in the middle of June.

The next day, I packed my bags and left the hotel room I was so familiar with in Accra. They always gave us the same room when I was over. We made our way to the airport and I wondered if this was the last time I would leave here alone or would I have to come back again to visit my own husband. It was scary. We were just married and most couples are beginning their life at this time. We knew what we had to do and we had known all the way that it would be hard. It was hard to say goodbye to my husband when I just wanted to hold him forever. He was much more used to having to do hard things to get by and he took it all in his stride.

For some reason I wasn't really upset. Each time I came back to Ghana I felt a little more secure in the future with this man and my affiliation with this nation. This time, we were married so I knew, no matter what, we would have to be together now. I had decided in the back of my head what I had to do. People asked me at home:

'What if he doesn't get the visa'? I had said that I would move to Ghana and teach in a paid job and we would keep trying. That was another difficult decision to make but now that I had chosen to marry, he became the main focus of my life and I would do anything to be with him. For the moment I had to go home and work as we were broke after the wedding and the visa documentation fees. My boss was expecting me back anyway and I had certainly taken full advantage of my holidays.

We kissed, said see you soon, and off I went to the familiarity of Kotoka airport check-in.

I had such mixed feelings of elation, anticipation and hope. We had left it in the hands of God and we knew He wouldn't let us down.

We had done all we could and it was now out of our control. It was becoming more and more clear to me on this learning journey how little control we all have and it is so refreshing to know that it has nothing to do with us in the end. We can only make the decisions we think are best, remain strong and faithful and the rest is out of our hands. So that was what I was trying to do here. I was attempting to be strong, leave the sense of control and hope for the best.

I left Ghana and I arrived home as a married woman . . . . alone!

Chapter 18

The Waiting Game

My mind was consumed. How could I concentrate on my day to day life knowing that my husband was so far and without any idea of how the visa process would go?

There was no guarantee that he would get the visa, even if he was married to an Irish woman. We just had to wait. They had said it could take from 6 to 8 weeks but I was checking my emails every day anyway. When we were waiting for the visitor's visa 2 years before, I remember checking my email every day in frantic hope. Then, one day, I opened it up and there it was:

'We regret to inform you that your visa application has been denied'

It is a terrible feeling and, this time it would be worse. There was more at stake now.

The weeks passed and we spoke on the phone everyday supporting each other and keeping our spirits up.

It then dawned on me one day . . . . what if he does get the visa? I had to think of the other side of the coin. He would be living in Ireland with me and I wondered how it would go. Where would we live? I was living with my friend in a rented house and I was struggling financially as it was. The country was in the depths of recession and I knew that the prospect of him getting a job was very slim. What would he do every day while I was at work?

I decided that these things would come together as everything else had and we would cross those barriers when we got to them. I wasn't short of offerings of opinions from others either. Those around me never failed to bring up the stark reminder of the times in Ireland we had now entered. How on earth would my husband find a job when there were now over 400,000 people on the live register in Ireland (claiming social welfare payments while they are out of work)? The foreign people who had been desperately needed to work during the 'Celtic Tiger' were now leaving the country. Scores of Polish people who had taken up residency in Ireland were going back to their families. The government were refusing entry to so many as there were simply no more facilities for them. Now, suddenly, the jobs the Irish didn't want during the boom years were in great demand. The solemn mantra of 'they come over here and take our jobs' was back with a vengeance. It had disappeared for a while when there was full employment and we were grateful that the Indian guy was working through the night in the local petrol station and Anna from Poland was serving in the bar on a Sunday morning. But, now, it was different. We wanted that work again and as the solid pensionable job with benefits became something of the past and was replaced with the 'contract hours' concept, the country was shifting. My family worried about the welcome or lack of it that Kwabena would receive. If he did get a job, how would it be perceived? The Ireland that my generation had so greedily been fed no longer existed and we had to accept it. I was confident that evolution would yet again unfold and we would learn to live in our surroundings however poor we may become. I wanted to do it with the presence of the man I loved and I knew we would get through the initial hardship.

Then there was the worry my family and friends expressed regarding how our relationship would be viewed, how we would be treated. It was definitely more common in Ireland now to see an inter-racial relationship but perhaps not as prevalent as in other European countries. Mixed couples still proved to be quite a head turner and, I myself often stared when I saw a white woman with a black man or vice versa. My father, who visited Dublin city once a year for his Christmas shopping certainly didn't agree that mixed relationships were common in our capital. He thought we would be alone out there in the Catholic, potato eating population and he worried for us. I tried to put everyone's mind at rest during this period. This was never going to bother us. Irish people had come a long way on the journey of immigration and tolerance. Of course, people may comment but they do that anyway, whether a person is overweight, spotty, cleft palate among many other things. It was so clear in my mind that I never felt the need to defend my relationship. Defence served a purpose which signified doubt and insecurity. Once you found yourself in a position where you don't have to defend something even if it is being criticised, then you know it is right for you. Those around me were never critical or insulting, they were simply concerned and acted in a loving way. I did share some of their concerns but I had to keep believing that it would work out somehow. There was a greater power leading us in the right direction and He would take care of us somehow even if we first had to live in the depths of despair.

For the moment, I tried to get on with my work, continued to write and do normal things trying to keep my mind occupied and focus on the positive outcome.

My parents continued to live in far more anxiety that us. I could see my mother struggling with the whole thing. She spoke to her sisters and all kind of conspiracy theories emerged. He wouldn't get a visa because, perhaps, he has a criminal record. Perhaps, we had made a terrible mistake and there is no chance if him being in this country. My father was reading every article in the paper relating to immigration and inter-racial marriage. They were all, of course, negative. There were Eastern European girls marrying Nigerians in the country so they could get residency. This was all coming out now and there was a worry that perhaps we would not be accepted.

Apart from all that, I was beginning to focus my mind on how we were going to make a cross-cultural relationship work. A culture is made up of a bundle of views and beliefs in relation to sexuality, war, law, religion, politics, social behaviour. In our own culture, we form a basis for how we look at all of these things and how we apply them to our everyday lives. Some of us venture outside of them sometimes, or outright reject them but, generally, we as Irish people accept certain norms for what they are as part of our make up. We understand that humour can be used at the most unlikely of moments (deaths, funerals), that if someone buys a round in the pub it will eventually come to you and you will get a round in. We know we are almost expected to complain about politicians, the weather, the price of houses and bankers. We come together as a group to do that. The list is endless. If you were born in born in France, you would rarely buy a round in a pub. Food would be more important than a beer with the lads. In Germany, work ethic is more culturally acceptable then being a very 'outgoing person'. So we use our world around us to define us as a culture. We may also respect that others have different cultures and that is fine. We sometimes do not always like the belief systems in other countries but we still accept it. We have ours and they have theirs and that's what makes the world such an interesting place.

Now, when we have to penetrate the other's culture to be allowed in and break up some of our own systems to let them in, it becomes a different kettle of fish. In my world, homosexuality may be acceptable. In their world, it may be an abomination. Women may be treated differently. Humour may not exist in the way we know. Religious beliefs may take precedent over 'doing the right thing'. It would be a challenge for anyone entering the world of cross-cultural love and it would be no different for us. I looked forward to the challenge!

The days passed and, admittedly, the tears flowed. It was difficult at night when I imagined myself lying beside my husband and waking up to his lovely face in the morning. He didn't seem quite as perturbed as me but then his faith always proved to keep him so strong in the face of adversity.

It was a Tuesday morning in the middle of August, almost 7 weeks since we had handed in the papers to the Irish embassy in Accra. I was in the office with my boss preparing the timetable for the coming term. I had my email open (which I never normally would in work but given the circumstances!). As my boss was speaking I saw that a new mail had come in and I could see it was from the embassy in Abuja. Abuja, which is in Nigeria, is where the documents are sent from Accra to be processed.

My heart was racing and I started to sweat. The words of my boss drifted into oblivion and I finally told him I had received a mail and I needed to look. He left the office and I found myself staring blankly at the screen unable to open the mail. After all the time waiting, I now didn't even want to see what they had to say. Ridiculous!

I finally opened it and I only read 5 words but that was enough:

'We are happy to inform . . .'

My heart skipped a beat and I felt a sense of exhilaration I had never experienced before.

I immediately called my husband and told him to sit down as I had some news for him. He had never expected it to come through so quickly. He was so used to disappointment when it came to getting breaks. We had also discussed how it may take forever and the possibility of it not happening so this was a very pleasant surprise.

We screamed and shouted over the phone, well, I screamed and shouted and he calmly said that plans needed to be made and that he would see me very soon.

He needed time to sort out his business there and gather his things. We booked the flight for the beginning of September, 3 weeks away.

It was such an exciting time but it was also a time filled with slight trepidation and anxiety. There were so many things going through my head and I had no idea how anything was going to work out. Everything could be sorted out if we are willing to work at it and/or fight for it. There may be suffering, fighting, crying, anguish along the way but I knew it would come with laughter, growth, friendship and love. The balance had been enough up to now and I would continue to stay positive that this would continue. I had amazing support from most people. I still knew some whispers behind my back were coming to their peak now. It was against the odds and some in the land of begrudgery would never truly accept that I had married a black man. There were those who questioned my family regarding my lack of respect for my fellow Irishman.

'What's wrong with the Irish men?' 'What is she thinking—he is black'. It was like they had discovered that he was black and I had neglected to notice the colour of my husband's skin was a few shades darker. While I didn't defend nor need to defend the loving relationship I had found myself in, as these people were family, I did need to attempt to put their mind at rest.

Regarding Irish men, there was, of course, nothing wrong with them. I had been in relationships before which were fine but clearly not meant to be. It had nothing to do with the nationality; it was to do with where my heart led me. This is quite a distant idea for some Irish people and it was hard to grasp. We are a nation who succumbs to the wishes of those around us. We are used to saying what people want to hear, to doing what is right by the family, or in some cases, the church. It is not enough to follow your heart. You must think about those around you. You must think about what is the right thing to do. We can see the consequences of this kind of thinking in the number of divorces, unhappy marriages and domestic violence cases across Ireland and other parts of the world. I wanted to stand up for myself and do what I felt was right by me. I didn't know if my marriage was going to work out either but I felt I had as good a chance as any! A happier me would surely make those around me happier!

I explained that skin colour was not an issue for me and that if they could see past his skin, they would adore him. Not convinced. Some people would never accept the situation and I would live with that without any problem. I just needed them to be civil to my husband when he arrived and avoid racist slurs which of course they would never partake in. It was much more of a passive racism which is rampant in this country.

The first week passed and I set about cleaning the house thoroughly to allow space for my husband. My friend lived in the house too and it would take quite some adapting for us all to live together. I cleared out a wardrobe which I felt was a wonderfully selfless step!!

I put some Ghanaian paraphernalia around the house in the hope that he would feel more comfortable and awaited the impending arrival.

The day finally approached and I chose to go to Amsterdam to meet him on the transfer of the journey, partly to pass the 6 hour wait he had but mainly because I couldn't wait any longer!

Even though we were married, there was always this sinking feeling that I didn't really know this man. Talk about doing things the wrong way round—marry the man, live with him, get to know him! What a risk.

Armed with these thoughts and a sense of hope and positivity, I disembarked at Schipol airport and immediately I saw him. I sighed a sense of relief as I hadn't really believed that he would make it here until I could see it with my own eyes! There he was, in front of my own eyes, his black skin glistening in the backdrop of the European sun. Not for a moment did this man look like a duck out of water. He looked like he had been on European soil all his life and I knew there was hope that he would adapt and not want to take the next plane back to the African terrain.

We sat at that airport for hours and talked about everything under the sun. It was great, we found ourselves on the same page of this unpredictable book.

We agreed that the first thing we would do is drop our expectations. This would prove harder for me than first thought.

Anyone who has ever been I involved in a mixed race relationship will relate to the following issues which were dealt up to us during the first few months of this new life—one we entered blind folded, perhaps our vision distorted by the excitement of something different, perhaps over ambitious and thought we could show the world that this was acceptable and, even, better.

The first thing I tended to do was worry that he was going to be happy here. It never left my mind that I could be abandoned as he looked around the recession hit wet terrain that was Ireland and booked the next flight back to Ghana. He tried to reassure me that he had made a choice and focused his mind on being with me wherever that may be. The seeds of doubt, which I had rejected on so many occasions, were getting water to grow as I started to question my own husbands' reasons for being with me. Was he willing to live in this country, far from his homeland and those he loved, just because of me? It was a question that seemed to haunt me for a long time. I never questioned whether it was the visa he was after. I had married a man of integrity and dignity and I knew that wasn't his style. I just needed to accept that his decision was made and he was in it for the long haul.

In true Irish style, everyone would wonder how he was coping with the weather! It was the only question on everyone's mind as they met this mystery husband of mine.

We arrived at the airport and it was wonderful that Fred (as he would now be known as this is his Christian name) was greeted by people he had already met and come to love. There were a few strange faces thrown in and, even, some faces of disdain. But, overall, he received a warm Irish welcome. The first few days were busy meeting people and setting up home. It was after that that it all got somewhat difficult.

That constant worry of how he was settling in constantly plagued the inner spirals of my mind. He assured me and reassured me but I couldn't help feeling something that he himself was not even experiencing.

I wondered how he really felt about me in the midst of my world surrounded by my tribe, the clan of people who he had spent brief moments with were now his only source of family. Again, he had made a decision and whatever would come with that, he would accept.

They were all the petty things that came with an inter-racial relationship. I thought they were the barriers we were to overcome but I was wrong. Something much more sinister lurked around the corner—expectations.

It is incredible in our own worlds, surrounded by our own people, how we somehow manage to acquire expectations beyond our control. When I first met my husband, I didn't expect anything (or, at least I wasn't conscious as to whether I expected anything or not) but now, here I was, with these ideas of what a marriage was, of what men had to do in a relationship. I had never been married before or been involved in anything really serious but now I had become the world's greatest expert on couple counselling!

The first issue relating to this raised its ugly head in the form of affection. In marriage people hugged and kissed, sometimes in public, a lot in the privacy of their own homes and especially in the bedroom. I knew before this marriage about the affection culture of African countries. They do not display affection in public and men do not have that need to constantly unload compliments, gifts and kisses on their wives. But, here, I was expecting my husband to hug me when I looked a bit off, kiss me every so often to confirm his love for me and certainly, to cuddle me at night before sleeping and in the morning after waking. He wanted me to accept that our relationship was strong and there was now no need for reinforcing something that had been sealed by vows and promises. We were in trouble!!

The tension was beginning to surface so soon into this crucial stage of our marriage. We both knew the importance of communication so we talked our way through it. We decided we would reveal the expectations and then let them go. I started to unveil another layer of my cultural conditioning. I had to accept there may not be candle lit dinners ready when I got home, that 100 red roses would not arrive at the door on Valentine's Day, that I would not be showered with compliments of how beautiful I was. However, I was not willing to drop all of these ideas or ideals. I needed a compromise as he did. I am an affectionate person and I wasn't going to spend our marriage on the opposite side of the room. So he began to peel back his layers of skin and under he found he could be affectionate and he came to like it. It was an amazing metamorphosis into a warm affectionate being who, never having experienced this in his life before, was now able to allow it to penetrate him. I fell in love all over again. There would not be candle lit romantic meals but there would be hugs when I needed them. At the beginning, he asked that I tell him when I wanted a hug and I believed that was fair. He found it difficult to be the one to instigate the affection so I would need to come looking for it. After a while he sensed the need in my eyes and, now and again, he got it righ,. He kissed me every time he left the house and when he came back, before sleeping and upon waking. I didn't need to be told I was beautiful everyday or that he loved me but perhaps when he thought of it!!. I came to admire him so much for taking on this new cultural layer. It was not easy but he knew it would make me feel more comfortable. He also respected my ability to adapt. I stopped criticising him for all the things he wasn't doing and started adding understanding to the recipe. Every time I felt an expectation arising in me, I released it to the point that I could see past it and right into what was really important. He had to do the same or it would not work.

Each day brought new challenges in those first weeks.

The major difference between the Western world and Africa is how people interact. Here, we see the relationship between men and women as very intimate, usually sexual. Over there, it is different. There is an appearance of an incessant wish to flirt, but in fact, most interactions between the opposite sex are related to friendships. Everyone wants to be your friend. Men tell you that you are beautiful (outside of marriage!), not to charm you into a date of a sexual encounter, but because they mean it and they feel it should be said. They genuinely see the white skin as something beautiful anyway, so even if you are not a supermodel here, you may well find you are quite the hottie over there!

People ask you for your number because they genuinely think you would be a nice addition to their group of friends just as accepting someone on Facebook is. It is difficult for people in Europe to trust that a member of the opposite sex really does want to build a friendship. I always found myself dubious about certain men when they insisted I gave them my number. At first, I declined and said I had no phone or that I would rather not give them my number. They looked surprised at this excuse and wondered what I didn't trust about them. After weeks of this, I finally decided to give out my number to some of my 'admirers' and I was pleasantly surprised that I would get phone calls inviting me to football matches, festivals and a voice just to ask how I am. Quite refreshing. It came to be the reason why I loved so much of the Ghanaian life, meeting people at these events, experiencing the world through their eyes. I was brought into families I was only vaguely familiar with, particularly parents of the children I was teaching. They would have me sit on the floor and eat from their bowl of fufu as if I was part of their everyday routine. This was all down to me deciding to give my number out.

I remember when I first arrived in Accra and I met the group involved with the volunteers who provided us with our 'host families'. While I found my own work there, I did rely on this organisation to guide me towards a family I could safely stay with. This organisation warned the volunteers not to give their number out, to avoid the men who gave them attention and to steer clear of socialising with groups. When I look back on that speech, which I absorbed intently back then, it makes me sad. I chose to ignore their advice and now I wonder what that woman would say about the subsequent marriage. I really didn't heed that advice!!

This idea of swapping compliments and numbers all became so clear to me when I was in Ghana observing.

Suddenly, the case study in my own home was different.

The first time we went out my husband stepped into his Ghanaian shoes and told some girls they were beautiful. They had stopped to ask us for directions in the centre of Dublin city on our first outing as a married couple. They were dressed up as is expected of young girls on a Saturday night. Kwabena simply said to them 'girls, you look very beautiful'. One of them looked at me in a sympathetic manner as if my husband was this womaniser and I was going to be duped throughout the marriage. The girls responded to the compliment by flirting with my husband and telling him he was 'hot'. He had no idea what this adjective represented in this context and when I told him the meaning later, we laughed together.

On another occasion, at a friend's birthday party, he asked a girl he had been speaking to for her phone number as he would in Ghana in order to build up a friendship base. I had encouraged him to meet people in Ireland, but somewhere in my subconscious, I meant men, didn't I? No matter how culturally tolerant you are or how much you strive to understand differences, the green eyed monster reveals his ugly head whenever he has the opportunity.

I tried with every bone in my body to be understanding but I couldn't do it. I began to insinuate that this was unacceptable but he had no idea why I was so irate about the behaviour. I knew I needed another approach. I explained to him the situation here and that those girls probably thought he was some weirdo from Africa trying to get into their pants. He was surprised but he could see clearly now that he wasn't getting the reactions he expected.

Issues of cultural misunderstandings continued to plague us for the first months (and we will always deal with them throughout our life).

Something simple like visiting peoples' houses is so different in both countries. It was something I had to get used to in Ghana and now I needed my husband to be just as adaptable in my country. As is custom for him, we would go to visit a family friend and, upon entering the house, Kwabena would find the nearest seat, greet the people being visited and then take leave. I explained that we approach the house, say our greetings, maybe eat or drink something and that we may stay the whole evening chatting. This would be very unusual in his land where visits last a few minutes and not much dialogue is exchanged, especially if the person is older than the visitors in question. I often sat staring blankly at the wall for 10 minutes and was then told it was time to go. It always amazed me. Now, we found ourselves leaving my sister's house after 15 minutes. I followed suit at the beginning so that he could ease slowly into our way of life. I knew rushing it would make him feel uncomfortable and achieve nothing. Instead, I explained to people in question to be understanding initially and, of course, they all were.

Another huge challenge for anyone outside Ireland, particularly, is the extent to which we express ourselves through dialogue! Not always dialogue representing the most important issues of society, but often quite trivial conversations centres around the weather, the price of houses or the soaps! Although he didn't say it in so many words, I believe my husband was perturbed and almost terrified by the amount of talking he was exposed to in those days (and still now). In Ghana, people do tend to speak a lot but only for a certain segment of the allocated time given to us in this world. They would all have a debate about a particular subject, usually political or sport related (in Kwabena's circle. Different social classes merited different dialogue as in all societies). After the debate had ended, there would be this silence, quiet time where people reflected on what had been discussed. He now found himself in a culture where silence was not known for being more lead than golden. He recognised how much fun we were and could not deny the obvious friendliness but this incessant chatting was difficult for him to follow. I felt uncomfortable at times when the subjects entered areas of unknown territory for my husband for whom I wanted all of this to make sense to. The last thing I wanted was for him to feel marginalised in any way. All he really observed throughout the whole assimilation was the amount we Irish talked!! He would eventually come to the conclusion that if he couldn't beat them, he would join them.

He began to read our newspapers, watch the Television and all its glory. He started to discuss our politics as if it meant as much to him. It was amazing how, in those early days, he blended in so well.

It wasn't long before he realised that some conversations were more acceptable than others. The long glorious debate about God, the meaning of the Bible and how we will be blessed and one day meet our Maker did not go down well with an Irish crowd in the boozer (pub) on a Saturday night. In fact, it didn't seem to be on anyone's agenda as a topic for great discussion. We had only a few friends here who we could discuss our belief system with and I was only starting to get into the whole thing anyway. In our own private time we liked to have debates on the nature of being and what our path in life was. I had to warn my husband that many Irish people were only Catholic by label. He soon realised as the majority of people we met were very quick to say they didn't believe in God. This was a shock for him at the beginning. He couldn't understand how they thought they were here on Earth and how they were going to depart from this life. He accepted this fate and chose to avoid the topic rather then enter the long tedious task of conversion. He would wait for the recession to really take hold and see if people reverted back to a God they had deserted.

Having come from a background that gained independence from Britain in 1957, he was under the impression that Irish people were also passionate about their independence and their country. He knew we were proud to be Irish so why were we so reluctant to discuss how distraught we were over the situation in Northern Ireland. He tried to extract the anger in a Ghana—like debate but most of our generation had no interest and seemed to think it was of no significance to them.

I have to say, that is partly my fault as I am politically passionate and am very concerned about how we came to be where we are as humans. As an Irish Republican, I am proud that we fought and won our independence and I do believe that we should acknowledge this and see Northern Ireland as an issue that merits debate (and not violence). Personal passionate debates that we would have would often spill out to our social surroundings only to be met with looks of disdain. This was clearly another no go area.

A conversation which Kwabena tried to avoid (and was becoming increasing difficult) was the talk of 'stress'. It was a new phenomenon for him and he found it difficult to watch people try to cope with this evil power that had captivated the nation. They didn't do 'stress' where he came from but it constantly rolled off our tomgues. You just accepted what was for you or not for you, focused on what you could do and moved on.

After getting through most of these issues with a certain level of dignity, we knew that our relationship was growing. We were growing together. We were able to accept our faults and we were willing to compromise on every corner. It was wonderful.

Then things suddenly started to crack.

It was the depths of the horrible winter in 2010 when the roads were covered in ice and snow from November to January. It was freezing and seemed to be constantly dark. Kwabena had come to enjoy the Irish banter, accept the food and settle in as much as possible. However, the cold winter days sitting in the house alone were not much fun. He had accepted that this would be the way of it for the moment but I knew he was unhappy. I was worse. I was constantly worried about him at home. Was he lonely? Did he want to go home? Was he looking for work? Was he cold?

I would come home in the evenings and he would be there looking slightly forlorn. It was heartbreaking. The prospect of finding a job was slim and now we had rent to pay for both of us.

He found some work with Concern, but being on the streets every day in the freezing conditions trying to sign people up were taking its toll and he got sick. He was constantly feeling dizzy and was diagnosed with vertigo very soon after. This meant leaving the job and continuing the pursuit.

We had our Irish wedding blessing around this time and another opportunity to show our love in front of family and friends, mainly people who couldn't make it to the wedding in Ghana. After this, it all changed.

I started to suspect suddenly that my husband was cheating on me. Instead of rationalising anything in my head, I began to hurl the accusations at him, sometimes on the phone from work or sometimes when I came home.

At first I thought it may be Internet cheating or maybe he was meeting someone secretly. I then moved on to the fact that he had another woman in Ghana. I began looking at his Facebook page and became more suspicious at the messages of flirtation I was met with. When I confronted him, he was surprised. He thought I understood how they interact in Ghana and I had never behaved like this before.

The final straw for him came when I called him from work one day accusing him of wanting to sleep with a particular girl he had been chatting to online. He was so angry with me and told me he had had enough and perhaps we had made a mistake.

What was happening? I was about to lose my husband over this jealousy that had suddenly taken over my mind. It was not me and I couldn't understand why I felt this way. We talked about it and he agreed that we would try to work through it but he pleaded with me not to make him feel so bad by calling him when he was alone at home and accusing him of crazy things he knew nothing about.

Christmas came and I was feeling terrible. I had constant headaches and I could not stop crying. My poor husband was getting scared!

Then, it dawned on me. What could possibly set hormones off to such a degree that a person actually goes mad?

It was then I did a pregnancy test. As I held the gadget in my hand and saw the second redline appear, a million things went through my head. The first, however, was that it was going to explain the madness that I had succumbed to in recent weeks. I was also so happy as I never thought I would ever have a baby. We had discussed the fact that we may have a childless marriage and he had gracefully accepted this. It was always a bit of a bone of contention for me because I knew African marriages were usually topped off with an abundance of children. It was something I struggled with on a daily basis thinking of adoption and treatments we may need in the future. But here I was now with child!

When I told my husband, he too expressed delight at the fact he had not married a crazy lady but that I was pregnant and that would explain the mood swings! He was also so happy that he would be a father. We celebrated so much that day and, apart from the elation associated with having a baby, that day we grew closer together. Our relationship strengthened considerably and since that day we have been so strong. We put our troubles behind us and focused on getting ourselves together before the baby came.

Within the space of 4 months, Kwabena found a job, we moved into a 2 bedroom apartment, bought a car and decorated our nursery!! How life can change in the blink of an eye.

So, here we are now, this present day, living together and growing with the additional responsibility of bringing up our beautiful baby girl. She is the product of a mixed race relationship and she seems to attract attention everywhere with her dark (much lighter than we thought) skin, big brown eyes and, of course, the wonderful head of fluffy afro curls which are undeniably her most astounding trait.

The birth of our daughter brought us closer and it has brought those around us, who may have been sceptical at the start, to really embrace the love we have for one another.

We will bring our daughter up to be part of both the cultures she comes from. She was born in Ireland and will probably go to school here but her Ghanaian heritage is equally important. We will take her over as often as we can and her father continuously speaks to her in his native tongue—Twi.

I am now working as a college tutor of French and Intercultural Studies and our daughter goes to crèche during the week. Kwabena works hard hoping one day to start his own business again like he had in Ghana. People still ask me a lot if he is really settled and happy and I tell them his life is with his family now and there is no question about that. If we did ever decide to part, it would be for reasons cited in most separations—lack of communication, taking different directions or lack of trust. I don't believe it would be from our different cultures getting in the way. I like to think we have established understanding in our marriage and respect for one another.

My life hasn't exactly turned out as my subconscious mind thought all those years ago. But then, I was following a particular road and I am glad I stayed open to difference and embraced it. Looking around I see many people who are very content with their lives, but I see others who chose the route society wants for us all. And I see that they have settled for something much less than they could have achieved. This is the situation I chose not to find myself in. I had to make very difficult decisions along the way and the road I chose was long with thorns and thistles spread among the green grass and flowers. We are still racing, racing towards acceptance, sometimes behind and sometimes ahead but always moving. I have no idea how our life will be and I don't really want to see ahead. I just want to try and enjoy the moments. We have the challenges of most marriages and we have the joy of most families. There are days when it is all so difficult but so many more that are wonderful. I just have to look at our little girl to know something fantastic emerged from the road I was on. It is a road I will never regret taking.

Acknowledgements

T his book was really a diary I was keeping so that I had somewhere to express my feelings about all that was going on. My decision to have it published came from a long line of people encouraging me to tell my story as they found it very interesting and brave. So I took on the task of making it into a personal story which I hope will show others that sometimes hard decisions can be very rewarding and that having negatives ideas about others can be a good thing if we work through them and ask questions.

Some of the people who stood by me during all the madness that was the last 4 years of my life are the most wonderful people I could ever know. My parents are at the top of this list and I hope my references to them during my story have done them justice. I thank them so much for everything they have done. Along with them is my whole wonderful family who have been great. My friends, particularly Lisa has been a pillar of strength when I thought I was falling apart at times. My 'girls' Aed, Carolyn and Jen really crossed bridges for me and I appreciate that more than they know.

My colleague and friend Leticia Agudo was instrumental in putting the final piece of work together and I would like to thank her for that.

Finally, a big thank you to my husband who offered me not only support throughout but also invaluable information on Ghana and the customs and to my baby girl who has been the inspiration for everything I do. Thank you Anabelle Nana Akwia Yeboah.